KINDERGARDE: AVANT-GARDE POEMS, PLAYS, STORIES, AND SONGS FOR CHILDREN

KINDERGARDE

Avant-garde Poems, Plays, Stories, and Songs for Children

Edited by
DANA TEEN LOMAX

Black Radish Books
2013

KINDERGARDE: POEMS, PLAYS, STORIES, AND SONGS FOR CHILDREN

Black Radish Books
Lafayette, Louisiana
www.blackradishbooks.org

Many thanks to the writers in this anthology for their inspiring work. Thanks also to Steve Emrick, Una Lomax-Emrick, Anna Lomax, Danna Lomax, Debbie Flowers, Chris Smith, Patrick Maloney, Peter Merts, Sarah Anne Cox, Norma Cole, Nicole Brodsky, Sarah Rosenthal, Jennifer Firestone, Kristin Palm, Erin Wilson, Lauren Schiffman and Mark Latiner, the Jagger-Wells family, Laurie Brooks, Lisa Noble, Nicole Mauro, Marthe Reed, Susana Gardner, James Maughn, Elaine Ervin, Hollie Stanaland, Margaret Stawowy, Jill Harris, Mollie Cueva-Dabkoski, Heather Woodward, Joanna Sondheim, Judy and Natu Tuatagaloa, Daniel Ishofsky, Samantha Giles, David Buuck, Frances Phillips, Jean Wong, Louise Steinman, and the Coleman Elementary class of 2012 for all of their support and enthusiasm for this project.

Special thanks to the Creative Work Fund, Small Press Traffic, and Black Radish Books for their collective spirit and support of this project.

Book and cover design by Wayne Smith
Drawings by Cliff Hengst
First Printing, 2013 in the United States of America
Copyright © 2013 Dana Teen Lomax

ISBN: 978-0-9850837-6-2
Library of Congress Control Number: 2013931786

CREATIVE**WORK**FUND

Supporting New Work by Bay Area Artists

The Creative Work Fund, a program of the Walter and Elise Haas Fund supported by The William and Flora Hewlett Foundation and The James Irvine Foundation.

small press traffic
literary arts center
at **cca**

Helping writers break the rules since 1974

Please check out Small Press Traffic at www.smallpresstraffic.org
1111 8th Street
San Francisco, CA 94107
kindergarde@gmail.com

Dedicated to
Una, Cisco, June, Marissa, and Nikaya
with love

Table of Contents

Editor's Note

Dear Young Readers,

Welcome to *Kindergarde*!

Since this is an anthology of avant-garde* work especially for children, I've been thinking about the experimenting many of you do. A lot of you wonder about how the world works and often try out new ideas and possibilities. Sometimes your imaginations get you into trouble, and other times they get you a prize. Sometimes your experiments are mild, and sometimes they go too far. The writing in this book is like that too.

It has been a challenge for me, as an adult, to know just what to say to you about the experimental writing in *Kindergarde*. But I have thought of a few things. Here is what I've noticed:

The writers in this anthology try to be themselves and write in ways that make sense to them—even if they have to make up words or rearrange sentences or scramble up the page or forget punctuation on purpose or change the way a story can go.

These writers spend their time closely looking at and thinking about things. Like many of you, they wonder about the world and what could be, what might be, what's real.

They take creative risks. They commit to their strange ideas.

They don't always do as they are told or follow the instructions about how to act on paper or in society. They remind us that there are lots of ways to be.

I hope you enjoy this book! My daughter thought you might want to add your own pieces to *Kindergarde*, so we've included a few pages at the end for your writing. Have fun!

Yours in experiment,

Dana Teen Lomax
Mom & Poet

Are you wondering what avant-garde *might mean? Some adults disagree about the exact definition, but the Merriam-Webster Dictionary people say* avant-garde *means "...new or experimental concepts especially in the arts." That definition fits with how I see the writing by the artists in this book.*

HERE YOU GO

Johanna Drucker

Who is A?

Is A

a fat mAn?

Or

perhaps a glAm bAnd

from a very strAnge lAnd?

Or is a
a leAn womAn All slender and tAll

to whom everyone else looks exceedingly

smAll?

Is a a bAd cAt

in a fAnciful hAt

too busy to chAt chAsing mice with a swAt?

Or is a something else totAlly out of hAnd,

a crAzed clAn

of strAnge plEAnts

in a cAn of pAle sAnd?

Or a bAg that sAgs till it turns into rAgs

that are sw*a*rming with *A*nts cr*a*wling up someone's p*a*nts?

Is a p*A*rt of a n*A*me that's the s*A*me, a small hint of f*A*me,

whose f*a*ce would look perfect inside of a fr*A*me?

Or is a a b*a*th full of wr*A*th

or a cl*A*ss gone to m*A*ss

moving off very f*a*st

while a bl*a*nd b*A*nd on a st*A*nd

makes itself very gr*A*nd

and a tr*A*mp sl*a*ms a m*A*t with a very d*a*mp p*A*t

and then makes a pl*a*n

that ends in the tr*A*sh

till it st*a*nds

on its he*a*d

and turns t*a*il

with a sw*A*sh.

Who is *A*?

Charles Bernstein

Emma's Nursery Rimes

Glow Worm!
Glow worm!
Make your mother squirm!

Big Bug!
Get out of my jug!

....

Scribble, scrabble
Inner, outer
Who knows left, right
Cat flew off with a Bumble Bee
Now it's almost night!

....

Bounce the ball
As bounce can be
Sing a song
But don't bounce me

....

Silly Billy
Can't see me
Don't make me
Cry again

Saw the ocean in a rolling pin
Let's play on the jungle gym

....

A day at the beach
Is a peach of a day
To run & sing & play
We'll swim 'till 4
And go home for some snores
Then go back to the beach again

Joan Retallack

On Sasha's Words
Mew Belly Hat

I want to mew like a cat.
I want some jelly in my belly.
I want some jelly on my hat.

Oh Oh

Is that my belly mewing at my new red hat?
Is that my hat mewing at my silly jelly belly?
Is that my cat hiding in my big green hat?

jared hayes

from **fiftyfarms**
for harry smith

the chicken the cock the
cow the goat the horse
the owl the pig the
rat the sheep the wolf
the chicken the cock the
cow the goat the horse
the owl the pig the
rat the sheep the wolf
the chicken the cock the
cow the goat the horse

Vanessa Place

YES/NO

above below
admit deny
alike different
alive dead
always never
animal human
asleep awake
bad good
below above
best worst
black white
boy girl
brave afraid
busy lazy
busy resting
child grown up
cold hot
cry laugh
cry whisper
day night
destroy create
divide unite
divorce marry
dull fun
dull sharp
easy hard

exactly approximately
exciting boring
fail succeed
false correct
false true
forbid allow
funny serious
future past
future present
general particular
gentle rough
give take
go come
go stop
happy sad
hit miss
hopeful hopeless
hot cold
ignore notice
in out
intentional accidental
interesting boring
jabber keep quiet
jacent standing up
jumping sitting
kind cruel
know don't know
kiss kick

late early

lazy busy

lie stand

lie truth

like hate

like love

little big

loud quiet

major minor

miss hit

miss catch

moon sun

more less

negative positive

nice awful

nice impolite

nice nasty

not yet now

nothing everything

now then

odd even

odd ordinary

often sometimes

often never

other same

peace war

polite rude

public private

pull push

push pull

question answer

quick slow

rainy sunny

refuse accept

reply question

right left

right wrong

sad happy

safe dangerous

salt sugar

same different

sharp blunt

shut open

sister brother

special ordinary

stupid clever

subtract add

suspect trust

sweet sour

synonym antonym

take give

take off land

take off put on

teach learn

there here

tiny huge

together apart
tomorrow today
tomorrow yesterday
true false
under over
upstairs downstairs
unite separate
useful useless
useless useful
vacant occupied
valley mountain
very not very
violent gentle
voluntary compulsory
waste save
weak powerful
weak strong
well ill
white black
work play
work rest
worse better
worst best
wrong correct
wrong right
xeric rainy
yes no
yesterday tomorrow

young old
zoo zookeeper

Kit Robinson &
Flora Beatrice Breitbard

The Happy Onions

My music with the loud noise of happy onions

My blue night with stars on its outfit twirling in the sky

My prince with white sparkles on his jacket standing on a black carpet

My necklace with green chicken bones and rainbow chicken bones

My noises with orange and pink air

My good night with the blue nobody

My black and white mittens with purple people

My, my, my wheels of lonely doors

My, my, my school in Berkeley

My, my, my, my, my friends are in a play – called Christmas in Springtime!

Evie Shockley

Freedom Comes in Fuchsia
(A Child's First Mesostic-Abecedarian)

Once upon **A** time, three minutes

after thirty-three to **B**e exact,

a freedom **C**at fell, screeching

and clawing the win**D**, out of the otherwise

clear purpl**E** sky, and landed right

at Monica's **F**eet. It was a normal day, like

every other **G**udsday. Monica

had already done **H**er homework

and was beg**I**nning to write

a poem about **J**ellybeans filling

the fish tan**K** (a list of all

their cool co**L**ors: moo-brown, striped-

daisy, neon-su**M**mer, etc.),

whe**N** a yowl

and an explosi**O**n of fuchsia fur frightened

her into dro**P**ping her

brand-new **Q**uill pen into a glass

of cookie juice. It sho**R**ted out, of course

—on her very fir**S**t use!

The freedom ca**T** immediately

apologized. "B**U**t, but . . . cats can't

talk," Monica said, "E**V**eryone

knows that." "**W**hy not? I'm free

to e**X**press myself any way

I choose," the kitt**Y** laughed, adding two new

hues to Monica's **Z**any list of jellybeans.

Kenneth Goldsmith

Chapter 1 from *No. 111 2.7.93-10.20.96*

A, a, aar, aas, aer, agh, ah, air, är, are, arh, arre, arrgh, ars, aude, aw, awe, Ayr, Ba, ba, baa, baaaahh, baar, bah, bar, bard, bare, barge, barre, Bayer, beer, bere, beurre, bier, bla, blah, Blair, blare, blear, bleh, blur, boar, board, Boer, boor, bore, bored, Boz, bra, bras, Brer, brrrr, bur, burr, C.O.R.E., ca, cah, car, card, care, caw, cha, chaar, chair, char, chard, chaw, cheer, cheere, Cheers, Cher, chiere, choir, chord, chore, Claire, claw, clear, cleere, coeur, Coors, cord, core, corps, course, craw, crore, cur, curr, curs, czar, d'or, da, där, dare, daw, dawed, dear, deer, derre, dire, diur, door, dor, dore, dour, draw, drawe, drear, droor, duh, dure, dyere, e'er, ear, eere, eh, Eh?, eir, 'er, Er, er, ere, err, eyr, fa, få, fair, faire, far, fas, faugh, fawe, fayre, fear, fer, fere, ferre, fier, fiord, fir, flair, flaw, fleer, floor, flour, floure, foiah, for, för, force, Ford, ford, fore, fors, four, IV, foure, fra, frere, frore, fur, fyr, ga, ga', gah, gair, gar, gaw, gear, geere, giour, gnar, gnaw, goore, gore, gourd, grah, grarh, gras, graw, grrrr, Grrrrr!!, guard, gyre, ha, haah, hah, Hair, hair, här, hard, hare, harr, harre, haw, hawe, hear, heer, heere, heir, her, here, herr, hir, hire, hoar, hoard, horde, hors, hour, houre, huh, Huh?, hurr, hwor, ia, ier, ire, ja, jaar, Jah, jar, jaw, Jaws, jeer, ka, kar, ker, kir, kna, knar, knarre, knur, Kurd, la, La!, lair, lard, lare, laud, law, lawe, lawed, Lear, leer, leh, lere, lier, Loire, loore, lor, Lord, lord, lore, lough, lourde, Ma, ma, mar, mare, Mars, Maude, maw, mawe, mere, mha, mire, mirre, moi, Moor, moor, moore, more, mors, moure, mwa, myre, myrrh, na, nah, nahhh, Nair, nar, nard, naw, ne'er, near, nerd, nha, noir, nor, nur, nya, nyeh, o'er, oar, oor, oore, or, ore, our, oure, Pa, pa, paar, paas, pah, pair, paire, par, pard, pare, paw, pear, peer, per, perr, perre, pers, pier, poire, por, pore, pour, poure, prayer, preyere, pshaw, pur, purr, qua, quaa, quaer, Quah, quaire, quar, queer, quire, R, r, Ra, raa, rare, raw, rawe, rear, rer, rere, rh, roar, ruhr, sa, saar, sard, sarge, saugh, saw, sawe, scar, scare, schmeer, schwa, score, scour, sear, Sears, seer, sere, serr, Shah, shard, share, Shaw, shawe, shear, sheer, shere, shire, shmeer, shore, shour, shoure, shur, Sir, sir, sire, slaw, slur, smear, smeer, smore, snare, sneer, snore, soar, soor, soore, sore, sour, spa, spar, spare, sparre, spear, spere, sphere, spoir, spore, spur, square, squaw, stair, star, stare, steer, steere, stir, stoor, store, straw, sur, sure, svår, swa, sward, swear, swere, swoore, sword, swore, t'a, ta, taa, tar, tare, Tarr, Taur, taw, tawe, tear, tear, teere, ter, tha, thair, thaire, thar, thaw, their, ther, there, they're, Thor, tor, tore, tour, toure, trois, Tsar, 'twere, tweer, Tzar, ugh, uh, Ur, ur, urr, urre, vair, var, veer, Vuh, wah, War, war, ward, ware, wear, weer, Weir, weir, wer, were, werre, wher, where, Where?, whir, whirr, whurr, wir, Wire, wire, word, wore, worre, wors, worse, ya, yaar, yard, yare, yaw, yeah, year, yeer, yer, yere, yheere, yoore, yore, you're, your, youre, yr, yre, Za, zha, Zsa.

Mark Latiner

So-and-So's Monster

Your monster's name (but please see below): _____

When you're born,
you're assigned a monster—a baby just like you.

It grows when you do, only even more monstrous.

Inside, it looks like something inverse to you,
so much so that even your dog can't tell you apart.
With you in mind, your monster makes its way in the world.

If you will grow to be tall, so will it, and if you will grow to be small, it will too, but such qualities don't matter to monsters, who can stretch their limbs like rubber bands or shrink themselves boneless, a giant octopus slipping through a pea-sized crevice.

When you wore diapers, it wore diapers, only too loose.

When you walk, it walks, only much slower and with arms (if they exist) outstretched.

In the fall, your monster dresses up like you and yells: "I'm a human being!"

In school, monsters act rowdy and profane as their teachers look on with approval. The monster students scratch the chalkboard with sharp things like horns or teeth, often inscribing—accidentally—the answer to some high-level math problem.

All monsters possess perfect intellects. They use technology like they were born to do just that, with gusto and precision. They know just what to say, all the time.

Eventually, your monster will sit at a desk and think, or jump out of planes (without a parachute), or simply sell things to other monsters while wearing a name tag:

> So-and-So's Monster, Sales Assistant

> (The most kindhearted child will give its monster a name.
> The cruelest child will as well. Ambivalent kids tend not to.
> Their monsters are called "So-and-So's Monster.")

Your monster will make you feel important if you let it.

Monsters grow only to a certain age. Then they get younger until they grow old again.
Thus monsters may or may not be like the universe itself.

So think of your monster often.
Or don't. It doesn't matter much,
because when you finally meet your monster
(probably on a Thursday or the following Wednesday),
you will be older and it will be younger.

Maybe you'll be the cruel one, and it so very nice,
and it will open the door for you, and you will be shut, just like an unread book.

Or maybe you'll shake hands, shake your heads,
turn around, and head
home.

Rodrigo Toscano

Feelings

icky feelings school
in good feelings neighborhood

icky feelings white bird
makes scared
icky feelings yellow bird

spooks out
icky feelings brown bird

looking & blinking

*

good feelings fountain
in icky feelings mall

icky feelings ice-cream man
with good feelings smile

good feelings ice-cream cone
with icky feelings sprinkles

good feelings yellow birds above
laughing at
good feelings white birds below

good feelings brown bird

in the fountain

*

icky feelings grown ups fighting
in good feelings toy store

icky feelings music playing loud
in good feelings costume room

ha!

these are my dark green glasses

this is my long black cape

these are my new red gloves to touch

special buttons

secret powers

alphabet

sounds

my poem

Samantha Giles &
Jonas Brash

Untitled

rain taps on roofs
rain taps on windows
rain taps on cars
rain taps on houses

we take this music gently
it whispers to us in water
a song we know as our own
a song we sing together

we hide inside
pajamas warm
you keep us from dressing
you keep us from washing the day

the sidewalk is a drum
each drop a beat
this dance of weather
this melody of rain

drip drop splash
raindrops in a puddle
that's on the street
in the street there's a hole
where the rain lies
in the street

puddles:
  you make a
    dangerous bath
  for worms

invisible but to the trout
lying thirsty in riverbeds
and the glittering slugs
ready for sliming

i love rain
it taps on my window
and it taps on the roof
i love rain

rain is a song to me
rain is a song to me
it's not scary
it's not harmful
rain, rain is a song to me

Juliana Spahr

Everybody's Performance Art:
Ten Possible Reenactments

Jumping Piece, after Marina Abramovic

This is a durational practice. Everybody jumps up and down for as long as they can, in whatever form they want.

•

Shoot Piece, after "Shoot" by Chris Burden

Everybody is given foam dart guns with foam darts and is invited to shoot at everybody.

Tearing Piece, after "Cutting Exercise" by Yoko Ono

Somebody comes out dressed in a paper shroud. Everybody tears the shroud off,
one person and one tear at a time.

•

Undressing Piece

Everybody takes off their clothes and hands them to somebody else who then puts on the
clothes until everybody is dressed in somebody else's clothes. Everybody then walks around
the room as somebody else.

Body Pressure Piece, after "Body Pressure" by Bruce Nauman

Everybody should press as much of the front surface of their body against the wall as possible. Everybody
should press very hard and concentrate on the image of pressing very hard. Everybody should think
about the various parts of everybody's body, which parts touch and which parts do not.

Hide and Seek Piece, after Yoko Ono

Everybody attempts to hide in plain view until everybody forgets about everybody.

All Together Piece

Short strings are tied around the ankles of everybody. Everybody then attempts to walk across the stage.
When somebody falls, they stay fallen. Perhaps a domino of falls will happen. Perhaps not.

•

Water Piece

Everybody has a cup. Someday has a cup that is full of water. The somebody with the cup of water pours the
water into somebody else's empty cup who then pours the water into somebody else's cup who then …
This is done until there is no more water left.

Peace Piece

Somebody points gun or bow and arrow or something like that at somebody else. Or somebody fake hits somebody. When hit, instead of falling down dead or pretending to be hurt or angry, everybody runs up to the person who hit them and gives them a giant hug or a kiss.

•

Bed Piece, after "Bed-In" by John Lennon and Yoko Ono

There is a giant bed. Everyone is invited. There is no audience.

Thanks to Jonas Brash, Mina Benham-Cunningham, Nicole Geller, Lua Ginsberg-Portugal, Katie Linnenkohl, Una Lomax-Emrick, and Sasha Spahr.

Andrew Choate

Worm Work

A Dog is a Wolf is a Dog

Sometimes my sneezes
       smell like my dog
after he's rolled around
       on a rotting bird carcass -
I think it's a good thing.

Parasites are just really good questions
       that bigger bodies can't answer -
Why am I made of coagulated fishfire?

My blood is not the same color
       as the green that falls out of a kiwi
sliced perfectly in half -
       I could still be alien.

Frog hiding in an orange and mango pie
       cooling on the counter,
comfortable.
       Sticky eyes glazing
just above the crustline -
       Tidbit ribbit lick.

Put a fish in a glass
Wear it for a watch
A wrist wash fish watch
Water bubble time notch

The hands of time are antennae-whisker-fins.

Very Sophisticated, Like Intergalactic Velcro

Paper onion paper opinion
Onion paper opinion paper
Opinion papers paper onions
Paper paper onions opinion
       Taper on caper ion pap
       No tea, see: ape near nap
       Pin peer pire app rap rope
       ripe pie in rear pan tin ear

The Aptitude of the Pickle

Stands up straight
Glistens for company
Shakes hands in a way that you'll remember
Respects elders
Doesn't talk back
Cleans room
Wakes up early for school
Appreciates chores
Plays well with others
Dilly!

Global Navigation Firsts

When I first started rocking, I didn't know where it would take me. But I knew I had to keep going. I rocked and rocked, back and forth, forward and backward, moving my body like a giant pendulum – swinging my legs, bending my knees, jutting my chin, arching my shoulders, leveraging my neck, throwing my torso into each and every rock. In my rocking chair, I rocked.

But where was I going? East, it seemed: against the sun. Up it came, and towards it I went. By the middle of each day, I gave it my back - straight ahead no matter what. I rocked in my rocking chair across rivers, fields, railroad tracks, citrus groves, parking lots, busy intersections (thanks for stopping!), forests and home gardens - I think you can still use the kale! - until I came to the ocean. I knew when I started rocking I wasn't going to stop, but I had no idea I would rock so hard and so thoroughly that I would find myself at the edge of the continent, staring at that seemingly infinite expanse of water.

I made the decision, right then and there, to rock myself across. The first solo TransAtlantic Rock-Across. Picking up my knees, I gave a few practice swings, felt ready, lurched into position and, with my biggest rock yet, splashed on top of the water. I was off, rocking on water. My rhythm was solid; I used the crests of the waves to make leap after leap. My jumps got bigger and bigger too, so I started doing backflips in the air and high-fiving sailors on the decks of massive boats I rocked past. I finally came onshore in Casablanca, Morocco: I had just rocked the Atlantic!

When I arrived, I knew the next thing I had to do was rock the Pacific. So I did. I rocked around schools of tuna and slalomed through the Hawaiian islands like they were Pacific popsicle sticks. Barely catching my breath, there was one trek left: a circumnavigation of the earth in my rocking chair.

It was easier crossing the oceans this time, though hitting the antipodes on time and crossing the meridians at the proper designations made the voyage a little tricky. I still rocked it. Now I'm back home in Rock City, Illinois. I've rocked the world, all over the world, and everybody keeps asking me: what are you gonna do now? How are you going to follow up your rocking of the globe?

I just figured it out and you're gonna be the first to know: for my second act, I'm going to hammock my way around the planet.

Duriel E. Harris

The Feast of Now Town Sound

Now and now and now and now
begins the feast of now town sound.
Hear nearly near and farly farly far
the ear-ly echos eck and oh
and mime a riddle boomerang

in a cul-de-sac, like the U in sound
and the double U's in now and now
and then (and now), where WHAT unwound
and silly HOW tap-danced around
in the hospitable house of WHO.
Huh?

Such questy questions are of the kind
that set up shop in my ever mind
all day and night and yad and thing
like sticky songs that a frog might sing
crossing see-saw seas on an airplane swing.

Who fluffs white clouds for sunny dazes?
Or plumps them up with mayonnaises?
Whose thruways are endways?
Whose sidewalks are sideways?
Who measures the highways to make sure they're high?

Who nightly knits sleep's soft snugly socks
and guards the schoolyard's thatchy rocks
and adds the ANDs in the and-shaped spaces
and chisels the NOs on my parents' faces?
Whose unopened boxes of steps make staircases?

And when "Ice cream, too!" meets shrieks at school
and show-and-tell spells chocolate flakes, who
licks the icing off the cake
to prove it isn't waterproof?
Or some such silly window ledge?

Whose goofy grin grows in my bed?

Nicole Mauro

Chickens and Eggs for Nina and Faye

The thing is chickens
and eggs. Surely you've had
to have heard
one has to
have to
come first. For example, when
I was your age
I was your age,
and when you
are my age
you will have been
someone else's age,
and will understand why the adults like to say
"it's not like it's the first,"
and be as surprised
as I am
about eggs.
All I can say after all this time
is they are hole-sized, and
awfully likewise
in shape.
Same thing with hearts. I have
one. The thing is I know
I have one...one has to to be alive.

When
someone suddenly opens
it, and I am always sure
at that time
it's the first,
and am
surprised
that I am thinking that
at the same time
I am hurt.

Now you understand first
and the same,
why the adults
sometimes separate
yolks from their
eggs. They are just likewise
to chickens
that way.

Claire Blotter

More Quinoa

for Breakfast

Quinoa come to the
party   or quinoa not?
Quinoa   always
quinoa   to come   quinoa's
mom   quinoa's   when no
one else will he quinoaed
all the way home   and now
quinoa's gone   someone—
quinoa perhaps?
A watering   can   to quinoa
to quinoa's   lawn

Douglas Kearney

Douglas Kearney PREEEEESENTS

THE WORD: PLAY

A WORD-PLAY of WORDPLAY

You choose what lines to say! There are so many ways to play this Play!

A WAY TO PLAY THE PLAY

This part of the page
is **THE STAGE**
where the play
is played.
And this part
of the stage
is the page
where "**PLAY**"
is displayed.
Throughout this play,
PLAY plays
and some of the play
of the play
is with how PLAY
is splayed.

This part of the page is **THE LINES**
where you'll find words to say
when you play the word-play
called **THE WORD: PLAY.**
The lines are fair game
in this game that we play
in this play that's a game
of plays.

Below a stroke,
here you'll see
—or is it hear, you'll see—
things to make
the scene seen
or **THE SEEN** heard
or the scene herd.
It won't be hard,
you'll see. Things
have a way of coming
into play in a play.

The sides of the page
beyond the strokes
are **THE WINGS**
where things wait
to engage the stage
which in this case
is the page.
The things in the wings
clamor and murmur.
The waiting
and waiting
is too much to take!

PLAYe

RoLe

who's
Will!?

you
don't
say..!

say
don't
you..?

Will's
who?!

Re

bTAYK

I will say call me K
I will say call me J
I will say call me A

Those are some parts to play in this
part of the play.

A me call say will I
J me call say will I
K me call say will I

Play the of part
this in play to parts some are those.

ACT ONE: K **PLA**Y s THE **GRAY**

K saw the gray day and thought:
what a fine gray to play!
And then: rain, like the gray itself drained!
Rain on the concrete walkway was playing
a gazillion tiny xylophones. K sang
the middle parts. The wind did the _low._

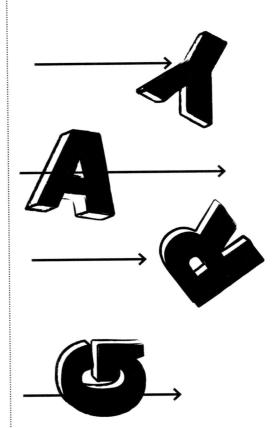

Gee, it's raining hard.
Are you sure that's rain?
Looks like letters to me.
A-B-C letters, you mean?
Why, yes.

ACT TWO:
J PLAYs AWAY THE GRAY

J saw the gray day and thought:
what a sluggy, ugly wet day to play in.
J wished to kabosh the wash,
opened the window and pulled the drapes in,
took a deep breath and puffed at the gray
'til it flooshed and b l e w into blue.

(to floosh is to flush and woosh)

Gee, it's winding hard.
Are you saying
winding or winding?
Ain't they the same?
Wind *and* **wind**—
maybe kinda.

ACT THREE: A **PLAY**S IN THE **GRAY**

A saw the gray day and thought:
what a fine gray to go in
and imagined the rain was an ocean.
A played a fish who could splish through sky
and swim on the wind, flew through the blue
'til it was gray again!

Angelfish are fish with wings!
Are you sure?
Jeepers no, I'm not shore,
but the beach shore is!
Why oh why did I ask?

PART ONE  PART TWO

ACT ONE: HORSE PLAY

Horses play on the plains
all gilded with rye. It looks like the horses
run on the sun when they play. So many horses!
Their hooves are like drums. So many drums!
And the sky is bigger than anything.

Horseplay is
horsing around.

I thought that
was a carousel.

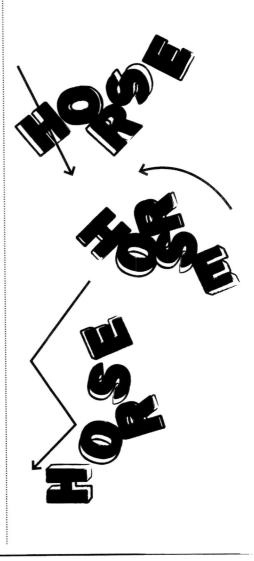

ACT TWO: HORSEPLAY

And under that bigger-than-everything sky
on the plains so gilded with yellowish rye,
one horse decides to ride another—
another horse pulls a horse like a wagon—...*MY WAAAAAAAAAAAAAYYYYY!!!!!*
And another of the other horses with hooves like drums
throws all its horse money at the one who will win—...*CAN DOOOOOOOOOOOOOOO!!!*

yYEEEEEEEEEEEHHHHHHHHHHAAAAAAWWWWWWW!!!

[HOLLER 'TIL
YOU'RE HOARSE!]

[SING THESE BITS
WITH UNBRIDLED GUSTO!]

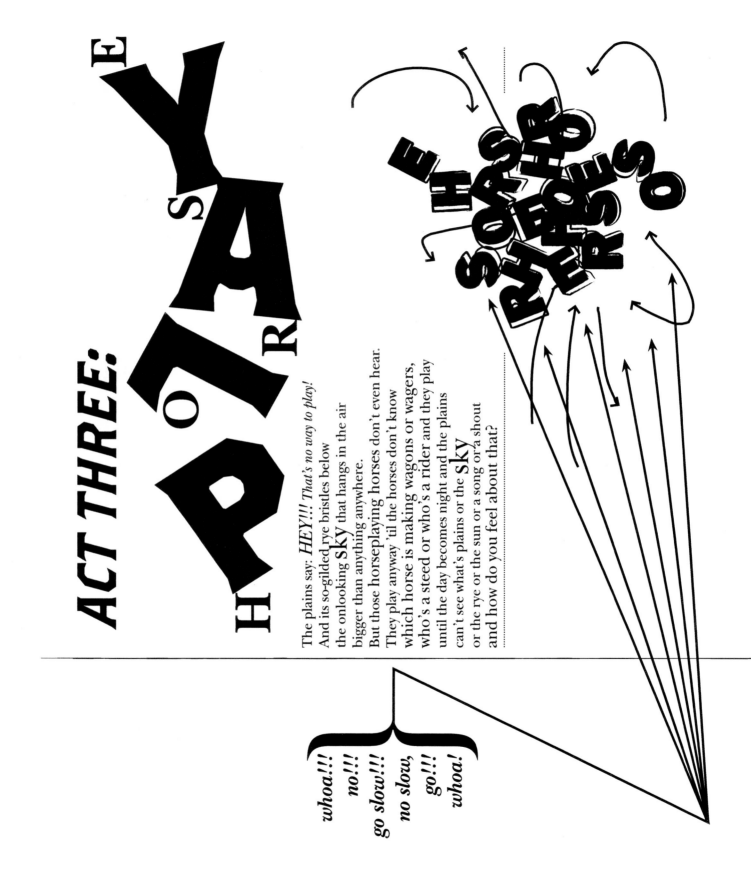

ACT THREE: HEYSPOILAR

The plains say: *HEY!!! That's no way to play!*
And its so-gilded rye bristles below
the onlooking SKY that hangs in the air
bigger than anything anywhere.
But those horseplaying horses don't even hear.
They play anyway 'til the horses don't know
which horse is making wagons or wagers,
who's a steed or who's a rider and they play
until the day becomes night and the plains
can't see what's plains or the SKY
or the rye or the sun or a song or'a shout
and how do you feel about that?

whoa!!!
no!!!
go slow!!!
no slow,
go!!!
whoa!

Jane Sprague

Lullaby Day-Jive-Rhyme
for Olivia

Dozens of leopards

          in a tree

Dozens of pelicans

          fly with me

Dozens of monkeys

          in a boat

Dozens of fishes

          swim the moat

Tens of diamonds

in a crown

Tens of cousins

skip around

Millions of morsels

for a mouse

Millions of feathers

flock this grouse

Jillions of cupcakes

                    spice my tongue

Jillions of laces

                    come undone

One cool Moglee

                    with a ball

One cool Moglee

                    runs the hall

Soft sleeping Silas

                           curls like silk

Soft sleeping Olivia

                           fine as milk

One love Daddy

                           rides down slopes

One love Mama

                           loops clay ropes

One sweet Dora

        spies a mouse

One strong Blue

        climbs the house

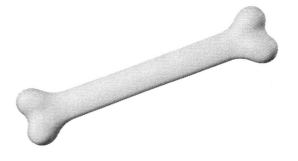

One kind Jasper

        floats on high

One kind Jasper

        whispers you a
        (doggie angel) Lullaby

Sawako Nakayasu

Battery

We get lost in the desert, lost very lost, and although we aren't going to tell anyone that we can't possibly be any more than two miles from civilization, the fact remains that we are lost very lost in the desert very desert, and the car very car is having a hard very hard very hard time getting started up again, and so we kick it very kick it in its "butt" very "butt" and the car is still having a hard very hard time and we are feeling lost all the more lost very lost in this desert very desert, and there is no one around us no no one very around us at all very all and there are birds very birds of which there are many very many, but the birds very birds don't know don't know how to help us and us and us help start the car very car and we are more lost more lost and we need help need very very help need very very help help and there is no no no one around us except if you count count count those ants in the ant hill that is all we have all we have are the ants very ants and then we wire them up yes wire them up yes I said wire wire wire and with the force of all the ants all wired all wired up and then on the count of three we all yell "CHARGE!"

Fear of Cold

For some reason, I am stranded in an extremely cold environment without my coat, and starting to worry if my life is in danger. After what seems like enough suffering has already taken place, I am fortunate enough to find a house, into which I break in and find a marginal amount of relief. There is nothing at all in the house, there is no power of any kind, and there is a large pile of dead ants near the bathroom door. I am a direct descendant not of MacGyver but his old-fashioned sister, and so I end up using my Other-MacGyver skills to weave a blanket out of the dead ants, which I finish as quickly as I can, and then throw over my body, begging it to bring me warmth. What happens is that I am so grossed out at the fact of having a blanket of ants covering my body, that I quickly grow both sick and intensely anxious about the situation, all of which nervous energy serves to cause the blood cells in my body to vibrate rapidly until I am quite warm, and stay warm until the weather goes warm and I am saved from dying.

7.9.2003

Ant-sized objects, in the order received:

Ant, microchip, staple, pine needle, dimple, pebble, the ant's twin, a one-to-one scale model of the ant, another ant of the same size, dust, crumb, fingernail, crumb, staple, mustard seed, the letter 'i' typed in 12-pt. font, the pinky nail of a 5-month-old baby (I'm looking at it right now), the hour hand of my watch, computer chip, an ant, a filling that's fallen out of your tooth, an ant, a word printed on linen paper that happens to be the size of an ant, a photo reduction of the cast portrait of an awful production of *Our Town* in Wisconsin, the back to an earring, the buttons on my cell phone, the bubbles in fizzy mineral water, staple, earring, tooth, the letter 'a,' the letter 'n,' torn-off cuticle, tiny glass splinter, eye-glass screw, cut-off hangnail, clipping from fingernail, stray "%&$#!" hair, un protozoaire, l'oeil d'un moustique.

I put them all in a glass jar.

I put my hand in and the ants go wild.

Camille Roy

Throat Bird

Miz Lucille	the teacher (5th grade)
Billy	a student
Gerta, Tina, Tom	students

Scene: a class room.

   Miz Lucille
(THWACK!!- Sound of ruler hitting a desk.) Don't just stand there. Take your turn!

   Billy
(Bent over as if gagging) B-b-buh. B—b-b-b-b-uh... B-B-B... Buh! B....

   Miz Lucille
Billy. Just. Say. It.

   Billy
COUGH, COUGH, COUGH, COUGH. Boy! Boy! *(Yelps as if in pain)*

   Miz Lucille
Everyone's waiting!

   Billy
   Boy h-has b-b-bird!!
   In t-th-th-the thrrrroat!
   B-boy has b-b-bird
   throat!

   Miz Lucille
Okay. Thanks Billy. Now class. Does this poem express a feeling? What is it?
(Class titters)

   Miz Lucille
(THWACK!!- Sound of ruler hitting a desk.) No giggling!

   Billy
   I had an attack of splash.
   Now the c-c clunk in the tongue
   is done.
   Now the throat bird sleeps
   in the word *'shush.'*

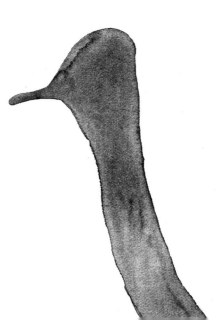

Miz Lucille
Thanks, Billy. You sure you're done?

Billy
Uh, no. D-done for now.

Miz Lucille
Okay, sit down. *(He doesn't sit down.)* Who else wants to read their poem?
(Hands raised)
Go ahead, Tina.

Tina
Billy didn't sit down.

Miz Lucille
(THWACK!!- Sound of ruler hitting a desk.) Billy sit down!
(Billy sits down)

Tina
Miz Lucille why does Billy say he has a bird in his throat?

Miz Lucille
That's called *poetic license*. Who can tell us what *poetic license* is?

Tom
It's a maginated license. Your magination makes the world. Any old way!

Tina *(mutters)*
I think it's weird.

Billy *(mutters)*
Y-y-you just think p-p-p-p-oetry is w-weird.

Tina *(firmly)*
Wierdo!

Miz Lucille
(Calling on Gerta, whose hand is up & waving) Gerta, what do you think?

Gerta
I have a poem. Can I read my poem?

Miz Lucille
Okay.

Gerta
(*Jumps up, acts it out*)
        Out in the clear
        I chase the monkey
        with my spear.
        In old style life
        it is very nice
        with ax and basket and knife.
        I am a very gifted wife
        In my oldstyle life!

Tina
That's a poem about chasing monkeys. Just sayin'.

(*Class titters.*)

Miz Lucille
(*THWACK!!- Sound of ruler hitting a desk.*) Class we are going
to applaud every poem. Let's applaud for Gerta's poem.
(*Everyone but Tina applauds.*)
Tina...!
(*Tina applauds clap, clap*).

Miz Lucille
Tina, do you have a poem to share with us?

Tina
Kinda sorta, Miss Lucille.

Miz Lucille
Okay, then.

Tina
(*Very slowly stands, pulls a paper from her pocket, unfolds it, peers at it, finally reads.*)
        There once was a boy named Fred.
        Fred had a hole in his head.
        He said to his mother
        I am like no other.
        She said, just don't leak in the bed!

(*Miz Lucille vigorously applauds, a few kids hesitantly join*)

One kid
(*loud whisper*) Tina didn't write that. Her brother wrote that!

Billy
(loud whisper) That p-poem is about Tina's brother!

(Class titters, Tina glares.)

Miz Lucille
(THWACK!!- Sound of ruler hitting a desk.) Silence!
(Class is silent.)

Miz Lucille
Thank you, Tina. That poem shows very good effort. Class, poems can paint a picture or tell a story or express a feeling. Did Tina's poem do any of those things?

Tom
It rhymed! Just like my poem. Can I read my poem?

Miz Lucille
Okay.

Tom
(Stands up, reads with relish)
    Looking for Rosalie
    Boy goes down by the tree
    and skins his knee.
    Looking for Rosalie
    Boy goes up by the cliff
    where he drifts.
    Boy goes watery cry-cry
    and makes the bridge sigh-sigh.
    Boy sings *I am a magic spinner.*
    I am a poet picker.
    I make the book take a look.
    I make time rhyme.
    But, where is Rosalie?

(Miz Lucille vigorously applauds, a few in the class do likewise, Tom beams and sits down. Beat. Tina raises her hand.)

Miz Lucille
Yes, Tina.

Tina
Miz Lucille, I still have a question. Billy has a bird in his throat. Why is that poetry and not, you know, Just Weird?

Miz Lucille
'Weird' is a label. It shuts people up. Poetry is the opposite of that.

Billy
(*Waving his hand*) Miz Lucille! I'm wasn't d-done! The throat bird almost c-come!

Miz Lucille
This is the last one from you, okay Billy?

Billy
O-k-kay! (*He moves to center stage and gets kinda bouncy on his knees as he does this next one.*)
 Words pile up in my t-throat
 words r-rub and they p-poke
 'till the bird floats into my thrrrroat
 and beats his wings while he sings
 and my throat hums
 and my lips trip
 and he flaps his wings
 and my throat claps and
 then I open my mouth
 and ow o-ow! COUGH COUGH!
 (bend over as if gagging)
 out o-out comes...

(*A person, probably a child, in bird costume bursts into view, who had been concealed at Billy's feet. The bird runs around, singing.*)

 Play with sound!
 The dazzle drizzle
 of the ground!
 The rains bake the plains
 with sheets of frizz!
 I'm word thing!
 I'm freedom ring!
 I'm the throat bird!
 I'm the throat bird!

(*The throat bird runs into the audience and out a door and disappears.*)
(*After the bird disappears, the kids cluster together and a few point towards where it went.*)

Miz Lucille
(*THWACK!!- Sound of ruler hitting a desk.*) Everybody sit down!
(*Beat.*
Kids ignore her.
They start to jump up and down, silently.
They are all out of sync.)

Miz Lucille
(*THWACK!!- Sound of ruler hitting a desk.*) That's quite enough poetry for one day! Onwards, to geography.
(*Beat.*
The kids get into the same rhythym.
This makes an impressive racket.
Lights down on the jumping kids.
Spot on the teacher.)

Miz Lucille
Pull out your texts, page 88.
Now who can tell us what happened in the last chapter?

(*Lights down, kids stop jumping.*)

Susan Gevirtz

Excerpted from **STREETNAMER ON THE MOON**,
a "collage" from the story of the same name

Streetnamer had known since she was small that when they started building on the moon she'd need to get there first. She knew better than anyone how much the name of a street decides what life is like on that street. What a challenge it would be to live on Jones Street or C Street. It was obvious that streets like that were named to save time and not to give the people any reason to come home to their houses.

For years Streetnamer had been preparing for the time when the moon would be readied for construction. In anticipation, she hid the space suit and alphabets in the secret chest in her closet. Still, she was horrified when, one night, she heard the official announcement on the late news waft from her parent's room through her half-open door. Triumphantly the reporter said that the crew of street layers had finished, and a network of fresh streets now waited on the moon. The authorities had decreed that the streets would be numbered. Numbered! That was even worse than she'd imagined. And so, immediately the next morning, before anyone was up she crept quickly and quietly to the roof. There she unhooked the Amelia II, which her parents thought was only a satellite dish for their TV, and floated up into the violet early morning sky before it was too late.

* * * * *

Weightless

The split second suspended above a trampoline

Before you come down

On a swing at the apex of the up slide

Riding a wave before

it breaks

        Helium-filled bodies coasting over continents

            like a rubber raft on a swimming pool

Blossom petal rain

  Book page in wind

 A complete change of plans

The flying fish before the net

The face before the mirror before the photograph

The egg whites before the waffle batter

The idea of you before you were born

     The taste of music   The shuffle of cards

The dresses hanging in the dark in the closet

The smell of fortune cookies

before their fortunes

         The smell of fires

    burning in the village where you will spend the summer

and the beach ball there before it's caught

Bathtub water cradle—closed eyes

Your dream inside of my dream

Your forgotten memory

                                        that I recall

        Your mother's fingers on piano keys

        sending you to sleep

A voice familiar as your own, familiar as the sound of water

        out of a faucet

        calling you home

Corn puffs on milk

Lace curtains on breeze

                        An avalanche of tumbling fog

        rushing in

The appearance and disappearance of the radio while you go fast down a summer road with

all the car windows open

                        Your car on rails gliding

                through a car wash

        The clock while you sleep

        A manta ray shadow

* * * * *

Taking half human, half gazelle steps, one second Streetnamer felt like a giant treading on the frail lines of a small child's drawing—the next she felt like an ant crawling over the vast surface of a game board. There were no other humans, no trees or buildings to tell her how she fit into the landscape. And the light that surrounded her was like none she had ever seen before. It needed a new name since it wasn't the same as the thing called light on earth. It seemed like a live animal moving around and changing the shapes and colors of all she looked at. Now it tilted, like a bird soaring to its left, revealing big cloud furrows and making the sky look as if it had just been ploughed.

Small streets emptied out into bigger and bigger ones until she found herself on a wide road that unfurled like a ribbon floating on wind far away out of sight. She stood for a long time looking down this road trying to see its end as it grew narrow in the distance. And when she absolutely could not see where it ended she took out a street sign and some letters in Baskerville and pasted *BOULEVARD of the BEYOND* on it. Then she hammered it into the corner of a side street and this main artery. She imagined that the people here might simply call it *Boulevard Beyond*, which was okay with her.

* * * * *

Continuing, Streetnamer gathered more speed. She called the next *Demanding Drive* and the next *Pancake Breakfast Place* and then *Yellow Yak Road*, and *Act Alike Alley*, next *Curlicue Curb, Cat Corner* and *Mirage View*, then *Quiet Close*, next *Dolphins Jump, Domino Drive,* and *Roaring Road....* On and on over the hills she scattered names.

When Streetnamer finally paused for long enough to scratch her nose, she thought she felt something moving underneath her feet. She stood still while the ground under her trembled slightly like a bird wing just before flight, but the ground didn't look at all like it was moving.... She bent down, closed her eyes and put her palm on the ground. Under it something was stirring or breathing and she imagined that her hand rested on the warm belly of a cat. Bending even lower she put her ear to the ground and heard what might be a heartbeat, or blood rushing in the big chest of the moon. With her ear to the ground and her eyes closed she remembered the way Polynesian navigators guided their canoes by feeling ocean currents through the wooden bottoms and up through their bare feet. And that's what it must be, she thought—yes, not an ocean under her ear, but an underground river rushing and arcing in wide curves below the precise angles of the bulldozed streets. What if she followed the river instead of the city grid work? What if she listened carefully with her feet to the places the river went and let that decide which street she came upon next, and next after that? Yes! That was exactly what she'd do! Starting now! And slinging her valise back over her shoulder Streetnamer set off into a rocky field in the middle of a city block guided by the river pulling her feet forward like the big pulse of an artery under the touch of one gentle finger.

For days Streetnamer continued to name streets. She followed the currents of the river that she heard like the crescendo of a silent orchestra under her. It led her to far corners of the uninhabited grid work and on out into the uncut terrain beyond. She wandered and listened, named, ate, watched and returned to the Amelia II to sleep and dream. Sometimes a street name would not come to her. She would put back her head and ask the sky for help and still only silence would answer. She would bend down and say to the river running invisibly beneath her, "Please, what is the name of this street?" and the river would keep its steady rhythm uninterrupted by her asking. So, once in a while she put up a street sign without a name, planning to return later, when the right name arrived.

Edwin Torres

THE NAME OF THINGS

Tell me a story about a frog named Painting and a bird
named Painting and how color changes color to see sky
Tell me about the fire that flies across a cloud called Rain
talk louder said my ear to my eye

Tell me about the time I saw you close up
and called you Moon and you point above and say
Sun visit me before I'm ready to play
and Painting bird me out of your way

Tell me about a feather called Girl and a girl
called Hair across the shadow of a day that won't sleep
And how things sound before they grow
did you know me before you saw me

Did you want the things you knew you couldn't keep
and the color that you grass with
And the light you shed your hair with
tell me about a girl named Story and a boy

Named Story who showed me how to talk inside my story
and the brush you use for fingers
And the tree that calls you Mine
tell me things I know but tell them how I know you

In the color of I know you Water colored me a bird
and Sky is what I bring you but Sky is just a word
Tell me about a yes named No and a no named Why
one day there was a painting said the ear into the eye

Beverly Dahlen

He was the Goat, I was the Girl

When I walked home from school
a different way,
not through town but down
another street,
I came to an old
orchard with black
scraggy trees,
and chopped down stumps,
but there
someone had staked a goat.
A goat! With sharp
little horns,
and a black and white
coat and glittery eyes.

I stopped. I watched.
I looked at the goat and
he looked at me. He was the goat,
and I was the girl
who watched
and watched
to see
what he would eat.
Would he eat anything?
as I had been told.
Would he eat thistles or
wood or glass or tin cans?
Would he eat worms
or spiders or cardboard or paper?
Ladybugs, ants or hornets or bees?
Strawberries, melons, carrots or peas?
Pudding or pie, cookies or cheese?
What would the goat eat?
Whatever one sees.
He ate grass. That's all.
Sweet green grass.
Soft grass. Chewing
and chewing
he gazed at me,
with his squinty
glittery
eyes.

Jill Stengel

this one.

the sun is waving goodbye.
the sun turned blue.

once upon a upon a time
there was a girl one. there was a boy one.

how do they live?   yes. that's it.
sit still. I'm telling you
                              the rest—

there is a house, of some sort
with walls. yes, walls. it could be a castle.
it could be. it could be another.

and sometimes a princess, and what will be her name.
sometimes a prince. and his name.

a castle, or a woodland cottage. a little house, rustic.
quaint. never an apartment, middle of the city. never
plain house amidst other plain. suburban tract perhaps.

this one could be different. a loft, a flat, uptown, downtown,
midtown, some town. somewhere.

somewheres.   there is a story.

once upon a upon a time there were or are
girl ones boy ones a city a home four
walls some time. or another.

once girl boy home time. an other.

once. other.
or another.

once upon a time there was a once upon a
      time the end.

once there was   (sung)   (to be sung)

once there were flowers and they grew, grew
    toward the sun, and they became a garden,
    and it, they, grew, continued to grow, reaching
    for the sun, as plants remember, as humans
    sometimes forget,
                            and there was a fairy (we
    forgot about the fairies!) and fairy waved the
    magic wand (wands!) and commanded or
    politely decreed or wished or demanded or declared
    for all the children, all the girl ones, all the boy
    ones, all the girlboy ones, all the boygirl ones, all
    the children—yes, all—whichever, however, and
    whomever they were or are or will be—all the
    children to do as flowers—to grow
    toward the sun—

(some fresh air. some walls. city, castle, wooded
glen. air, walls, sun.)

the children were frolicsome.
the children were quarrelsome.
the children were children, and did children
    things. in children-like ways.

often, a father.
often, no mother.
this story, a mother lives. and happily. kindly, not
    wicked nor cruel, and whether step- or plain ol-
    plain ol, she loves the children ones.

father, often misguided, sometimes foolish, usually not
    paying attention—this story can be different.
    this story can be your story, or my story, or
    anybody's story. daddy's a prince. daddy's a
    king. daddy's some guy, just trying to do his best.
                    and loving.

there are some walls. and there are flowers. anybody can
    plant a flower. some kind of flower will grow, almost
    anywhere. (not Antarctica. not outside there. C wants you
    to know that.) (he is sleeping, but he would tell you that
    if he were awake. I know he would. if he were reading
    this story as I write. or having it read, he would
    interrupt there. not in Antarctica. not outside. there.)

there are walls. and flowers. sky.

mothers.
fathers.

girl ones. boy ones. in between ones.
who cares what who wears?

a wand waves, and it is sparkly.
boy fairies. girl fairies.

any all or none ones may slay, tame, befriend, or even ride dragons,
     depending on the tale.

let me tell you a story.

once there was—

some names. a story. a song.

(three children, and magic, helped this one along.)

Jeanne Lance

Ode to a Toad

Oh fierce, bespeckled, pimply toad
who sits beside the ancient road
& talks to rushes slim & brown
your croak would wake the baying hound.
Oh toad when I look in your eyes
I see a prince for all your cries
'bout water, grass, & flies to eat
I think your hop, toad's, really neat!
In my youth when I was fair
I used to out the window stare
at the oval sink, the abode
of no other than sir & madam toad.
When I became most truly sad
& wished to raise my heart to glad
then down the steps & out the door
I'd prance like many times before.
To the toad pond I would hie
observe your back & squatted thigh
with my brother, younger half
we would whisper, plot, & laugh
& to the furthest end of pond
would haste to pluck a beauteous frond
to use as natural living brush
with which to lash your back, a rush.
& round about the pond we'd move
careful & stealthy not to disturb
too early, sleeping dreaming toad.
Then with a light brush on the back
into the pond they'd jump—
plop, plop, plop.

Reid Gómez

Slices of Bacon

Her boss, Rose, drops us off at the corner of 20th and Connecticut. We go into the butcher's. The Rodriquezes live upstairs. The butcher is a can of pop dough, I seen on the tv, all white and spilling out of his shirt. His apron is splattered red and pink. His eyes are cotton candy. He has a lot of meat in the glass case and a few things hanging from hooks. We ask him for our usual. He slices one half pound.

She pays with dollars she folds into packs. This packet for dinner. We take it home. Two tops of blocks, past Daniel Webster, past Linda's, straight down Mississippi. When we get there it's dark, both inside and out. We go upstairs and wash up. She changes her clothes to house clothes. I don't have but one kind so I stay like I am and get the breakfast ready.

When we get to get meat we eat like this—breakfast for dinner.

She takes her time and I go fast. I get the box of milk from the counter and the box of flour from the drawer. Water we got plenty of, hot and cold. I leave that to her. I get the bowl, she gets the rest. Real eggs we got yesterday from Mamacita's new chickens. No powder. I hate those. Everything that we gotta mix by hand tastes okay but eggs are always a disappointment. Scramblers, yuck. That means Star King. Over easy means Mamacita's.

Not today. We got even better than that, we got pancakes and bacon.

Fresh. We like it fresh. So, meat, we just get on occasion. Whatever it is we walk it home to cook. No refrigeration needed.

She's back.

She puts on the stove. We got a griddle in the middle. She sets it to start and gets her powders and her sugars. Butter we got in a little box, we collect it. She gets most of it at Tropical, the other ladies get them with their box food, but they never eat them. They give them to her.

Tonight is the night I learn the stitch you use for long and short texture.

One light. We use that. First for breakfast. I eat two pancakes as big as my face and three strips of bacon. Grandma eats her stack and we leave what's left for Norman. The grease we save for tortillas and beans. The rest we wash up. It goes fast. Cast iron don't need no scrubbing.

She cleans while I get my threads. My head don't even reach the doorknob so I sit on the sofa. My feet just reach the edge. The kitchen table is too big for me to sew on. I gotta see what I am doing.

We use thread that comes at the store. It appears when I'm not looking. I go through the basket and pick out my colors. No. 791 and No. 895. That's black and green for beginners. We have a pile of white cloth and I fish an old one out. Today is learning so I pick one that's used and put it in my hoop. She comes to sit down. We sit in an L. She's the long part and I'm the short one.

She takes her threads from the basket and grabs a cloth, the same size of mine. One needle. She takes four strands. I copy and split mine. She threads and I follow. No knots. I know that much. We leave our tails hanging out behind us.

She starts a stitch and I follow behind. She has her square. I have mine. She goes forward and backward. Her hands move on her lap and her eyes watch me as I try to do what she does. Looking back and forth like tennis.

We go like this for a long time and I try to remember two things. Don't sew down my cloth to my shirt. I do that a lot without thinking. The second thing is I'm making a shape. This is the stitch for setting out space, not for flowers. For flowers you gotta whole nother way. Making flowers is easy. You can use this stitch for petals, some people do, but I'm learning how to make lines and shapes.

She's got a pinwheel going around. The wind blowing it in circles. A north to south wind. She's pretty fast and she isn't even looking at hers, she's looking at mine.

My string is so long. The next stitch it gets short. I just keep on sewing. A few more in and a few more out. I need another thread. I start to get the scissors to cut two arms length. That's how you measure, an arm, two one knuckles, around the hand. It depends on what you're making. Sometimes we take our practice work out so it's better not to have a bunch of short pieces. I'm measuring a long one. Before I cut she says her first words.

"You need a new thread?"

Then she pulls up on hers. Never stop with your needle on the wrong side. 'Cause then when you start back up you might forget to sew up and start sewing around the hoop. Then you've got to take your needle out, remove the stitch, rethread and start over. It's better just to always stop with the needle on the right side. She pulls hers up and it's still about an elbow length long and she's got a complete piece. I just got an almost looks like half and a very short thread. Something's wrong I know.

She shows me her back. It looks like her front, except in reverse.

I show her mine. The problem is there. It looks like dibé before you cut their hair.

"What happened to mine?"

"You got knots."

I look at her like I'm dumb. I'm not, but I still don't understand. Hers is smooth. Mine is a mess.

At least it's not attached to my shirt. I haven't done that for at least three weeks. I keep looking. I know what comes next. Take the needle off and start pulling through. When I get to a knot, untangle it, never cut. I start. The first one comes out easy, the second, not so. I've got a pile as thick as a my uncle's hair.

She goes and makes a Red Rose tea which means I'm gonna be awhile. Patience. If you don't have it now, you will some day. The scissors sit in the basket. She drinks the whole cup. Finally my thread is one long piece of string, four strands. I put it back in the needle, careful not to split the thread. With all my pulling it's a bit of a mess. She tells me to roll it between my fingers. No spit. Spit is bad. I'm always sticking the threads into my mouth, especially when she's not looking. Use your eyes and use your hands. Mouths are for food and words. We don't need much of either.

She sits back down beside me. Our knees touch. She picks up her thread. Ready. Are you? I am. I pick up my thread and start making lines.

"You should know how much the thread is going to change with each stitch. If it's different then you have a problem."

She talks soft, past my ear. Right angles. We make them, with our bodies, with our threads. I understand.

"Mine goes from long to short real fast."

"Do you check your back?"

"You never flip yours."

"No. I can feel it." She doesn't flip, but I can see her fingers smooth out the back.

"When you get to the end it shouldn't be a surprise. You should know."

We keep sewing. I keep flipping mine over to make sure there's no knots. She finishes hers. I'm an almost done. Practicing takes work. I'm working mine through. My thread goes impossibly short. I'll never be able to weave it back. My Grandma just keeps sitting. I look at her and then I flip.

"I got a knot."

She smiles. Her face perfect, her eyes black pearls. Her glasses hang on string around her neck. Her sweater open.

I take off my needle and pull the thread through, undo the knot and rethread my needle. I'm about to stop to talk but then I remember. Never stop on the wrong side. I pull the needle up and sit. Thinking it through.

"It's good to check for knots."

"But you never get them."

"I used to."

"When"

"When I was like you."

I smile, thinking, she was never like me.

She folds her cloth and puts it down. I follow behind like I do. The street lights our room and I change into pjs.

No stories tonight. I think of my threads going smooth. I don't know her secret. She lays there awake till I sleep. My night is full of circles and squares. The edges take all my parts and put them into a picture. I keep it inside my head. We're not allowed to use patterns. They have those in plastic bags at Woolworth's on Mission. We work on white fabric and we work from our minds. This is the dream. I am dreaming.

Robert Glück &
Jocelyn Saidenberg

Precious Princess, or, PIG Speak

Photographs by Chris Komater

(Balso the Knight, Sleeping Beauty, and Sock Monkey run onto the stage in circles making high-pitched chirps, then stop abruptly in position. Monkey just lounges, silent, in boneless positions for most of the play. Players, please, talk SLOWLY like on a very lame children's show.)

BALSO: Sleeping Beauty, where is your head?

SLEEPING BEAUTY: Hello to you Balso the Knight. I don't know where my head has gone, Balso! (pause) It must be around here somewhere. (They both look.) There are so many things you can't do. I miss my hats. Where can I put my crown?

BALSO: You are still very beautiful, Sleeping Beauty.

SLEEPING BEAUTY: Of course I am! (posing a little) Show me YOUR best profile.

BALSO: Uh, do you think this is my best profile, Sleeping Beauty?

SLEEPING BEAUTY: Noooooo.

BALSO: How about this?

SLEEPING BEAUTY: I guess you don't HAVE a best profile, and I have TWO. But nobody likes me—everyone hates me. Everyone is jealous of me and hates me and I don't have any friends at all! (She starts weeping.)

BALSO: Oh Sleeping Beauty, I like you! I'll be your friend. Do you want me to be your friend?

SLEEPING BEAUTY (looks at him and shakes her head sadly, still weeping): No.

BALSO: You may not have any friends, Sleeping Beauty, but you look like you are ready to have a baby. Are we in Hole-ville?

SLEEPING BEAUTY: We were walking in Hole-ville and fell through a hole.

BALSO: A hole? Where are we now?

SLEEPING BEAUTY: Balso, we are in a Beautiful Country.

BALSO: What makes it so beautiful?

SLEEPING BEAUTY: Oh, Balso, there are napkins and flowers!

BALSO: Sleeping Beauty, are you going to have a beautiful baby?

SLEEPING BEAUTY: Yes, yes. I am going to have a precious princess. I am going to call her Precious Princess. She is going to be my precious beautiful baby.

BALSO: Precious Princess? That's a lot of p's.

SLEEPING BEAUTY: Oh, Oh, Oh, I think I am having my baby right now—here she comes! I can feel her moving inside of me. She is coming out, here she comes!

(Sleeping Beauty lays a very large egg.)

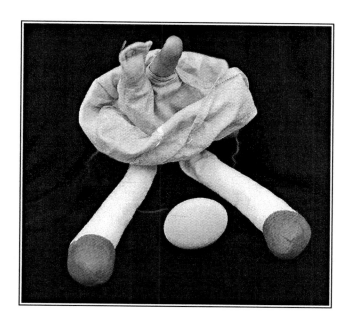

BALSO: Wow, Sleeping Beauty. I have never seen such a big egg. You may not have a head, but you have a big pink egg to hatch.

SLEEPING BEAUTY: Now we have to wait for my egg to crack. I am so excited! My precious princess is in my egg!

(Lights dim, sound of clock ticking)

BALSO: We have been waiting for a long time, Sleeping Beauty. I think something is happening, your egg is rocking back and forth. Your egg is making sounds like an airplane taking off, your egg looks like it is about to explode. Oh my, something pink is coming out.

SLEEPING BEAUTY: I am so excited! At last I will have a precious princess. Look, Balso, there's a pink toe!

BALSO: And a pink ear, too, Sleeping Beauty! What will you call her?

SLEEPING BEAUTY: Precious Princess, you moron! Here she comes! Here she is!

(Precious Pig emerges from the egg. Stretches, crawls around curiously.)

BALSO: Wait, Sleeping Beauty, that's not a precious princess. That looks more like a PIG.

SLEEPING BEAUTY (squealing): A PIG? A PIG? My precious princess is a PIG?

BALSO: Well, it certainly looks like a pig.

SLEEPING BEAUTY: Oh no! I wanted a precious princess, but instead I had a pig?

BALSO: It sounds a pig: oink, oink.

SLEEPING BEAUTY: My baby is a PIG?

BALSO: I am certain it is a PIG.

SLEEPING BEAUTY: Oh dear! I thought I was going to have a precious princess, but instead I had a PIG.

BALSO: There is no doubt, Sleeping Beauty. A Big Pink Pig.

SLEEPING BEAUTY: Is it possible? Is it real? I wanted to have a precious princess, but instead I had a big pink PIG!

BALSO: Is it true, Sleeping Beauty, what I heard long ago?—that your father was a pig farmer?

SLEEPING BEAUTY: *Who told you that!!!*

(Sound of clock ticking. They all turn and watch as Monkey gets up and elaborately changes positions. Precious Pig crawls back into the egg.)

BALSO: We have been waiting for a long time, Sleeping Beauty. I think something is happening, that egg is rocking back and forth. That egg is making sounds like an airplane taking off, that egg looks like it is about to explode. Something pink is coming out.

SLEEPING BEAUTY: I am so excited! At last I will have a precious princess. There's a pink toe!

BALSO: And a pink ear, too! What will you call her?

SLEEPING BEAUTY: Precious Princess, you moron! Here she comes! Here she is!

(Precious Princess is born. She crawls around curiously.)

BALSO: Wait, Sleeping Beauty, that's not a precious princess. That looks more like a PIG.

SLEEPING BEAUTY (squealing): A PIG? A PIG? My precious princess is a PIG?

BALSO: Well, it certainly looks like a pig.

SLEEPING BEAUTY: Oh no! I wanted a precious princess, but instead I had a PIG?

BALSO: It sounds a pig: oink, oink.

SLEEPING BEAUTY: My baby is a PIG?

BALSO: I am certain it is a PIG.

SLEEPING BEAUTY: Oh dear! I thought I was going to have a precious princess, but instead I had a PIG.

BALSO: There is no doubt, Sleeping Beauty. A Big Pink Pig.

SLEEPING BEAUTY: Is it possible? Is it real? I wanted to have a precious princess, but instead I had a big pink PIG!

BALSO: What should we call her?

SLEEPING BEAUTY: We shall call my baby Precious Pig.

PRECIOUS PIG: (Stands up, surveys horizon, claps her hands gleefully): Greetings, friends!

(Sleeping Beauty and Balso the Knight gasp and move away.)

PRECIOUS PIG: If you are my mother, than where is your head?

SLEEPING BEAUTY: My Head?—*missing*. (sighs) My head is with my Precious Princess—not here, but *elsewhere*.

PRECIOUS PIG: Mother Without A Head, or M. W. A. H. or as we say on the Continent, Moi.

SLEEPING BEAUTY: I am not Moi—I am the Royal Mother. No abbreviations, ever, Precious Pig.

BALSO: Delighted to make your acquaintance, enchanté, Balso the Knight.

PRECIOUS PIG: If you are Balso the Knight, where is your nest?

SLEEPING BEAUTY: PIG child, where DO all your questions *come* from?

PRECIOUS PIG: My pink precious pig pate possibly.

BALSO: Your pretty piggy piercing porcine patter pleasing platoons of paparazzi?

MONKEY: So says simpering saccharine suppurating soullessly slushy susurrating simpletons!

SLEEPING BEAUTY (indignant): Easy for YOU to say!

PRECIOUS PIG: Since I was born *with* a head, let's begin my education.

BALSO: Oh, er, where to start?

PRECIOUS PIG: Philosophy!

BALSO: The origins of meaning, of space and time. We can call it, Pigology.

SLEEPING BEAUTY: No, no, Precious Pig, I want you to grow up to fan yourself, wear my 12,000 hats, and put your napkin in your lap.

PRECIOUS PIG: Royal Mother, I want to learn about caves and shadows, but more than that, I want to roll in the eternal mud.

SLEEPING BEAUTY: You mean poetry? Let's have an elegant salon. Does anyone have a potted palm? There's nothing like a potted palm for culture. Let's recite poems. Is everyone ready? Me first:
(with a dramatic delivery)
There was a fair maid called Marie.
Marie was invited for tea.
I mustn't be late,
I simply can't wait,
I'm expected at the palace at three.

(They look at her in bewildered silence.)

PRECIOUS PIG: My turn! My turn!
(with wonder in her voice)
There was a young fellow called Nietzsche
Whose favorite dessert was the lychee,
There's no substitute
For this cute über fruit
Though a scoop of sorbet can be peachy.

(They look at her in bewildered silence.)

BALSO: May I recite a poem?
(in a very flat tone)
There was a young fellow named Fred.
Fred had a hole in his head.
He said to his Mother,
I am like no other.
She said, Son, don't leak in the bed.

(Sleeping Beauty listens with growing discomfort. Five seconds of bewildered silence.)

PRECIOUS PIG: I believe I can interpret this poem! It seems to me that Fred had a kind of wound, perhaps not a physical wound, but a wound to his psyche. The second half of the poem explores Fred's relationship with his mother, and I think it supports this reading. He is wounded and he is dying from it, and his horrible horrible horrible mother can only think about superficial things, appearances. She doesn't really care at all what happens to Fred. She is indifferent to her son's fate, or to the damage she may have inflicted.

(They are silent a minute.)

MONKEY: Allow me to offer an interpretation. It seems to me that Fred had a kind of wound, perhaps not a physical wound, but a wound to his psyche. The second half of the poem explores Fred's relationship with his mother, and I think it supports this reading. He is wounded and he is dying from it, and his horrible horrible horrible mother can only think about superficial things, appearances. She doesn't really care at all what happens to Fred. She is indifferent to her son's fate, or to the damage she may have inflicted.

SLEEPING BEAUTY, PRECIOUS PIG AND BALSO: Wow! That's Brilliant! What a mind! Amazing!

SLEEPING BEAUTY: I've heard about enough of this. It is true that your Royal Mother is missing her head. Even though I can't remember where that missing head might be, this talk of Poetry is making that missing head ache.

BALSO: Isn't it time for tea?

PRECIOUS PIG: I am hungry, Royal Mommy. Let's have some chocolate covered food.

(All leave except Monkey.)

MONKEY: (To the audience) At Precious Pig's age, self-preservation, chocolate and philosophy are the same things. Off they go, *exeunt*, who needs them? Or you? (To the audience.) Monkey lives in a Monkey world! There *is* no outside if you travel on the Astral Com-plane!

What's this?????? (He finds Sleeping Beauty's head and addresses it, as Hamlet does Yorick, while he sits on it, throws it in the air, etc.) Sleeping Beauty!—You think YOU'RE having a bad day. When I was standing in line at the bank, the man in front of me coughed! *It was horrible!!!* I felt like MY HEAD was going to fall off. Why are you torturing me????

You think YOU'VE written a play! You think YOU'RE in a play! You think YOU are YOU!!!! I have written, directed and starred in the movie version, play version, novel version, opera version, torch song version—you name it! I *invented* Pigology, before there were even pigs or even lologies. Jeez. I am all versions. Monkey Variarum Monkey, to be precisely Latinate. In Monkey where Monkeys make more Monkey and nothing more, Trippy! The critics made a big fuss when I starred in *Titus Monkonicus*, and when I was shot out of a cannon in *Monkeys on Parade*. (He speaks in Sleeping Beauty's voice.) "This is the very limit of anything that we ever saw or wanted to see or even could imagine." (sings) *Monkeys, on Parade! Talking 'bout Monkeys on Parade.* Hand to hand combat, death and desire, we all just want to be shot out of a cannon by one of our own kind. That is, *I* created the universe for *me!* I AM the expanding logic of the Empire, but take it from me, Sleeping Beauty, I am also the ambiguity that rules the depths.

(Monkey carries Sleeping Beauty's head off stage.)

Fin

Lyn Hejinian

A Tale in which a Prince falls from a Nest

This tale like many others happened once and only once and I will tell it only once and then no more so listen well and if you do you will understand why I have filled my basket with sand.

There is a small cottage halfway up a hill not far from a tree from which early one morning a prince fell from a sparrow's nest when he was still so young that he didn't know the difference between shadows and reality nor remember how or why or when he had become a sparrow and he never would, since no one can remember anything until they have lived for awhile and when one is old reality has cast so many shadows memory goes blind. This is why the history of the world depends on tales, which are like potatoes and have many eyes.

On this particular morning four beautiful girls had come out of the cottage to play and when the prince saw them he leapt into the air and landed on a branch in the sunlight. The girls' parents loved them dearly and had dressed them in brightly colored shirts and told them to beware of cats which in this part of the world are the size of cars and it is only because the cats are forced to wear bells on their collars that they haven't devoured every living thing for if they had you would not be here to hear this tale and I wouldn't be here to tell it.

Now listen well and if you do you will understand why it brings good luck to dream of a silver bucket in a yellow cart.

"We will name you Chip," said the youngest of the girls, "and bring you dishtowels to sleep on."

"We will bring you seeds to eat," said the oldest, "and also some raspberries."

"We will build you a fortress of sticks," said the younger of the middle girls, "and it will be your house."

"We will fetch water fresh from a faucet for you to drink," said the older of the middle girls, and now I will tell you their names since if you know those you will have a picture of each to see with your own two eyes and you will understand how it was that Chip the sparrow prince fell in love with all four. They were named Martha and Florinda and Alicia and Clair and they each hurried off to do as they had promised but when they returned Chip was nowhere to be seen.

Immediately Martha realized that no good book tells the same story every time it is read.

Alicia looked along first the south side of the cottage and then the east for the sparrow, and she saw some daisies and some ants and a caterpillar and a red doll's shoe. Florinda ran to the cottage's north side where the weeds and ferns grew in the shade and she saw some snails and a dented toy truck and a stone that because it was damp was blue. No one saw any sign of Chip.

Clair looked up into the sky and said, "Actually, I think Chip was a star."

'No way," said Martha, and she scattered the seeds she'd collected onto the path near the dish of water that Florinda had filled from a green garden hose coiled under a faucet near the back door of the cottage. Clair placed a folded dishtowel onto the ground under a tree beside the path and together the girls arranged some branches and cardboard over it. They set some raspberries among the branches.

That is the tale, and if you have listened well, you will understand that the four girls lived happily ever after.

Brent Cunningham

Young Willie Wonka

Characters:

MASTER OF CEREMONIES
YOUNG WILLIE WONKA
UNCLE HARROLD WONKA
EXECUTIVES

[Enter Master of Ceremonies.]

MASTER OF CEREMONIES: Greetings, friends large and small, friends medium and extra-medium, friends half-medium and a medium-and-a-half, and friends of every other size. I hope you are all ready to hear one the strangest, irregular-est, remarkable-est stories you have probably ever heard, not counting the stories you might have heard that are even stranger.

Many of you probably know the story of Willie Wonka and his Chocolate Factory. And you probably remember what happened to young Charlie Bucket when he visited the Chocolate Factory. But you may not know what Willie was like when HE was a kid, closer to Charlie's age, actually about the age of some of you there in the audience. Back then, Willie's uncle, Harrold Wonka, ran the most serious-est, most unhumorous-est, most no-nonsense-est candy company in the known world. It was called Level-Headed Candy Enterprises Incorporated. Young Willie Wonka, as you can all imagine, was VERY interested in all things candy-related, and he liked VERY much to go with his uncle to the candy factory whenever he could.

And THAT is where our story begins, at a top meeting of the Top Executives at Level-Headed Candy Enterprises Incorporated...

[Curtain opens on the executive offices of Level-Headed Candy Enterprises Incorporated. Enter Willie Wonka, Harrold Wonka, and Executives.]

HARROLD: Bill, Jim, Frank, Bill…you remember my nephew, Willie Wonka? I'm going to let him sit in on the meeting today. If I never have children of my own, one day Level-Headed Candy Enterprises Incorporated might be his, and it's never too early to learn how to manage a serious company in serious times.

EXEC 1: Very level-headed, Harrold.

EXEC 2: Very no-nonsense, Harrold.

HARROLD: Where's my other executives?

EXEC 1: Peter, Skip, Dave, and Bill are on their island vacations.

EXEC 2: Jim, Bill, Ron, and Jim are with customers at Disneyland.

EXEC 3: Ron, Skip, Bill, and Jim are with customers at Golfland.

HARROLD: Well, we'll have to do without them. What's to report?

EXEC 1: We've got new numbers, Harrold. Sales are down. We are in danger of going out of business. No one is buying either one of our candies.

EXEC 2: I agree completely with Jim. No one is buying our extra-dry, barely-sweetened Chocolate Bar Without Nuts, which comes wrapped in dull brown paper.

EXEC 3: I agree completely with Bill and Jim. Furthermore, no one is buying our extra-dry, extra-crumbly, slightly-yucky Black Licorice Stick, which comes wrapped in dull gray paper.

HARROLD: I see. What should we do?

EXEC 3: Sir, I was thinking…maybe it's time to make a NEW kind of candy to sell?

EXEC 1: A new candy? But we've ALWAYS had just the two candies!

EXEC 2: Yes, be level-headed!

EXEC 4: Yes, be even-keel!

HARROLD: Wait a minute, fellas. No one is buying our candy, right? So we need to listen to every idea. What we need are fresh ideas! Fresh thinking! What kind of new candy did you have in mind, Bill?

EXEC 3: Well, I was thinking of…a lollipop.

EXEC 1: We've thought of lollipops a million times. Lollipops are too whirly, too swirly, too twisty.

EXEC 2: Yes, lollipops aren't serious candy.

EXEC 3: Well, maybe we could serious-ify it? It could be just one color, like green. And it could be barely flavored, just lightly minty. It could taste like floss. And not too sweet either. Almost…bitter.

EXEC 1: Very business-like! It could be the color of cooked asparagus.

EXEC 2: Very straight-shooting! It could even taste like cooked asparagus.

EXEC 4: And we could wrap it in drab green paper!

EXEC 1: Very level-headed!

EXEC 2: Very even-steven!

EXEC 4: Very no-nonsense!

HARROLD: It sounds great, but how do we know the kids will buy it? Willie, how's that sound to you? (Willie shrugs.) Come on, Willie, tell us what you think.

WILLIE: I was thinking…what if the lollipop looped?

EXEC 1: What's that?

EXEC 2: How's that?

WILLIE: What if it looped up like this. And then it maybe went over like this, took a turn here, and came down here. But the stick was over here? So you would run over here and hold it, then you would run over here and take a lick, then you could turn it, and roll it like a bicycle. Then over here, then here. Then over here would have a bit of cake or jellybeans on it. And if you wanted you could get inside and ride down the street…

HARROLD: Willie! This is a serious candy company. We make serious candies for serious times.

EXEC 1: Very un-level-headed.

EXEC 2: Very un-clear-cut.

WILLIE: I've got other ideas. How about a candy robot? You could open the sides of his ears and steam would come out, and the steam would be cotton candy. And each time you licked it, you would go two seconds into the future, because…

HARROLD: Ok, ok, Willie, thanks for the ideas. Gentlemen, I think it's settled…let's start making the Lightly Minty Asparagus-Flavored Drab Green Lollipop starting tomorrow.

EXEC 1: Sir, there is a problem.

EXEC 2: Yes, we need new workers to make the new candy.

EXEC 3: And we can't get new workers because even the old workers…

EXEC 4: Aren't happy.

EXEC 1: I agree.

EXEC 2: I double-agree.

EXEC 3: I double-double agree.

HARROLD: What do you mean not happy?

EXEC 1: Well, it's hot down there in the factory, it's noisy, and we don't pay them very much.

EXEC 2: Not because we don't want to.

EXEC 3: But because no one is buying our candy.

EXEC 4: So there's no money. So they quit a lot. Also, we fire them a lot.

HARROLD: I see. What do you suggest?

ALL EXECS: We don't know.

(long pause)

WILLIE: I know how to make the workers happier.

EXEC 1: I think your uncle asked you to be quiet…

HARROLD: No, no…let's hear the kid out. How would you do that, Willie?

WILLIE: Well, there could be room with a snow-cone machine, and they could go inside it for break and eat snow-cones. And…if there was an amusement park at the corner that they could go to, go on a surprise, that might help. And after the amusement program there could be a museum of science nearby, and they could go to the museum of science to learn about science. You could let them watch a Bollywood grownup movie, and there could be a movie theater, and they could dress up as who they wanted, and act out something with a few other people. And they could go home at one in the afternoon just for lunch, or they could just say, "Hey, I'm going to go home and play a quick video game, be right back."

EXEC 1: Harrold, you're not actually listening to this are you?

EXEC 2: A snow-cone machine! Do you know how noisy those are? It's already noisy down there.

WILLIE: If there was a button that calmed it down you could press it until it was so quiet, like this, err, err, err. And then it would go pop, pop, pop. And you could put clouds over it. I could throw a hundred clouds over it to make it quieter.

EXEC 3: How could people go home for lunch? It takes them hours just to get here!

WILLIE: They could move to a house in the factory, made of candy, so that it was only like two inches.

EXEC 4: Why are we arguing with this kid? All his ideas cost money. And we already know Level-Headed Candy Enterprises Incorporated doesn't have any extra money.

EXEC 1: That's right, all the money is allocated.

WILLIE: What's "allocated"?

EXEC 2: It means all the money we have is already supposed to go to other places.

WILLIE: Where is it supposed to go?

EXEC 3: Lots of places!

EXEC 4: Right! Some of it goes to pay for Bill, Jim, Skip, and Harvey.

EXEC 4: Right! And some of it pays for Jim, Frank, Bill, and Ron.

EXEC 1: A lot goes to pay for Executive Vacations.

EXEC 2: Yes, a lot.

EXEC 3: And trips to Golfland and Disneyland. That takes a lot.

EXEC 4: That's right, a lot lot.

EXEC 1: We give a lot to ourselves as bonuses.

EXEC 2: And we give a lot to ourselves as bonus bonuses.

EXEC 3: And a lot of it we steal.

EXEC 1, 2, and 4: That's right! A lot we steal.

[Pause as everyone realizes what's just been admitted.]

HARROLD: Steal? Steal? Wha...wha...wha...GET OUT!

[Harrold chases the Execs around the office with a broom or other object; they run around like rats until they all exit.]

HARROLD: Willie, what am I going to do? I can't trust anyone. My candy company is broke. Who is going to help me?

WILLIE: Uncle Harrold, kids eat the most candy of everyone, right?

HARROLD: Yes, it seems like they do.

WILLIE: Well, I'm a kid. And you can trust me. Why don't you let me help you run the factory?

HARROLD: Maybe I'll do that, Willie. At this point, I don't see what harm it could do.

[Enter Master of Ceremonies.]

MASTER OF CEREMONIES: And that, my variously-sized friends, is how Willie Wonka began working in the candy factory business. Level-Headed Candy Enterprises Incorporated had lost so many workers they had to look around the world for someone who wanted to help make Willie's candies, until finally they visited Loompaland and discovered the famous Oompa Loompas. But that's a story for another day...for now I'll just say so long, and please try to remain the size you all are, no bigger, no smaller, and no medium-er.

Garrett Caples

Short Lives

scenes from the life of a toaster:

my bagel didn't gel
i can't read this bread
i went dutch on an english muffin
this pop tart is pop art (instead)

scenes from the life of a cellphone:

my call dropped cuz my caller dropped me
my battery died so you're in charge
oft i'm apt to opt out of my apps
in texas, they send tex messages

scenes from the life of a bellybutton:

blue shirt today!

scenes from the life of a shoe:

i think i stepped on something
i think i stepped in something

there's a hose in my shoe
there's a horse in my shoe

my toes are hoarse!

scenes from the life of a poet:

zzzzzzzzzzzzzzzzzzzzzzzzzzzzzz
zzzzzzzzzzzzzzzzzzzzzzzzzzzzzz
zzzzzzzzzzz—!??—zzzzzzzzzzz
zzzzzzzzzzzzzzzzzzzzzzzzzzzzzz
zzzzzzzzzzzzzzzzzzzzzzzzzzzzzz

scenes from the life of a television:

—we didn't have days back in my day
—no, papa, please...
—we just had nights, so we called them *nights*

[laughter, applause]

scenes from the life of a coaster:

drinks on me!

scenes from the life of a necktie:

knot again
snot against

i'm tied up right now
i'm tired of hanging around

blue shirt today

scenes from the life of a grapefruit:

i'm totally juiced for breakfast
i tend to take things in sections
no, i am *not* a fat lemon, thank you
could i squeeze in a little pulp fiction?

scenes from the life of a sweater:

your mother bought me for you
july is moth month for my closet kin
i come from a close-knit family
you can get pulled over in a cardigan

scenes from the life of an eraser:

i don't remember what it said
i don't have time to read every word
i don't do ink

are you sure?

i can't undo
this operation

scenes from the life of a mirror:

why are you staring at me?

scenes from the life of a coat hanger

my head hurts; my shoulders hurt
this blazer is making me hot
i'm all bent out of shape

blue shirt again!

Stephanie Young

POEM FOR KINDERGARDE

Some lines written after my friend handed me a stack of paper held together with a paperclip and I didn't know what I was looking at. There were pictures printed on the paper. The pictures told stories about kids. Sometimes the stories told kids what to do or how to feel. What not to do, or what not to feel. After I thought about this and looked at the pictures and felt confused I thought too many stories tell people what to do. Too many stories tell people what not to do, or what not to feel.

Sometimes I get up out of my chair and run around.

Sometimes these lines in the drawing
where I'm running around
and around mean I'm running
in circles around my family when
I'm supposed to be sitting down.

Everyone at the table has a bowl.
Everyone at the table has a spoon. I'm running
and they look confused and maybe
a little angry as I'm running I just
leave my bowl and spoon where they are.
My arms close to my body I'm trotting.
I'm trotting around the table. Like a horse.

A person going around tables with wide eyes, and kind of blank

my brother looks scared but my eyes

I realize all the people in this picture I'm looking at are a boy except the mother.

What's that about?

This is a poem about running around tables with high spirits.
Or this is a poem about a picture that says you should not run around a table
so many times it leaves lines on the picture of this experience.

You know what, run

*

Then I fall asleep inside, at my desk, with my head on a piece of paper.
Then I fall asleep at lunch, dinner, or breakfast. The sun shines through the window.
Then I fall asleep again. More paper, more pencils, more sun, more window.

*

Everybody went to school.
I ran the other direction with my backpack on.
I had this look on my face.
It looked like my backpack had—rockets! Or rocket blasters.

*

Here is a story. Two kids playing with a doll. Another kid
that's us running through the story with a trumpet.
Back and forth with a trumpet.
Over and over again blowing a trumpet.

*

I sat on a rock at the beach and felt sad.

That's what it felt like. When they asked if I wanted to join them I held up my hand, like
"Oh, no, I couldn't possibly."

That's what it was like. What it felt like on a rock.

I was at the beach.

"Oh no I couldn't possibly."

*

I tied—
no, I teased a dog. The dog tied to the wall.

*

Running and running again, winter and I lost my mitten
at home and I lost the pieces to the puzzle, they flew out of the box
at home in my slippered stockings
in my house with a game I lost the pieces of, also mittens

like rockets running with my backpack
that looked like it had rockets
the paper was flying
the paper and pencils

are you like that?

Also with cake and pie and cookies and soda. Then, my tummy.

The papers just flying?
The backpacks like rockets?

"Oh no, I couldn't possibly."

And that's what it was like. What it felt like on a rock at the beach.

It felt sad.

I thought about the same kinds of things. Thought about them in a bubble
above the character's heads. I thought about the same things
in bubbles. And that's what it was like.
The papers flying, and the trumpets, and the tummy.
I had this look on my face.
I went the other direction.
I kept looking up, away from the paper.
It wasn't great with the teacher. I don't know what
I was looking at. I put my hand up and said "4!"
really enthusiastically. "No, I couldn't possibly"
(that's the teacher) so I jumped back up
and said "5."

A little bit how
it was like.
Like reading.

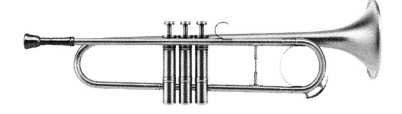

Cathy Park Hong

The Hula Hooper's Taunt

I'mma a two-ton spiker   hips fast rondeau
N'ere more, nay sayer   feel this orbit rattle

Wipe that prattle that spittle   crass pupa
Gupta   away you   ma' man,

where you   revolving   solving
spin shorty   shark satellitic   fever

Leer not, lyre   I spiral atom pattern
Faster than you say my turn.

Notes from the Historian:

We wandered into a stadium where thirteen hundred people competed for the national hula hooper's contest. The last one standing won the contest. While hula-hooping, they taunted their neighbors to discourage them. From your seats, you could not actually hear them but I snuck onto the grounds where I overheard the invective. I also enjoyed sitting high up on the bleachers to listen to the deafening rattle of thirteen hundred hula-hoops in action.

giovanni singleton

Tumble Rock

                                        sun
                                        punch

                                        rubber ball

                                        brown
                                        beach

crowded   heat
stoop   waves

jack rocks   hula hoop

                                  black
                                  top

                                  kick ball

                                                          city
                                                          walk

                                  hopscotch

june
air

                                  jump rope

                                        turn
                                        turn

                            faster   faster

Etel Adnan

A STORY: Sambouba and the Palm Tree

Sambouba had at last to go to school. She was going to be five years old, and it was time to do like the other children of Bagdad. Her parents persuaded her that she would play at recreation time with other kids her age. At the beginning she thought that home was a much better place, but before long she had plenty of friends ... to be a lonely child was not fun anymore. After a while she decided that she will take her palm tree along. Father said that it was impossible for a tree to go to school and learn to read and write. She resisted. Her tree was like no other tree in the world. When her father found out that she was crying, his own heart started to hurt. In the morning he decided to allow her to take her tree to school. She was so proud to have to show her little friends such an exceptional thing. The school mistress was surprised. She didn't know what to say. But she was sure of one thing, a class-room is no place for something so tall, so unexpected, so out of place. She became adamant. At best, the palm tree will have to wait outside, by the side-walk. Sambouba reluctantly agreed. That day, in the middle of the afternoon, just before the time children had to return home, a big explosion happened. This was a time of war. A bomb blew the tree to pieces. Sambouba had never seen anything dead. Her parents had to explain to her what war was about. Her father took her in his arms. They went together into the garden. He explained to her that war was the ugliest thing that human beings could do to each other, but he also added that as wars have to start they also one day stop, and no trees are again blown away so violently. She wiped her tears. Her father said: "Look, Sambouba, I will plant a new palm tree for you, we will do it together, you will help me."
Sambouba smiled, and from the window, her mother watched and felt happy about her family.

Brian Strang

Elizabeth Treadwell

the fairly cwen

the olden seas sweet edges
far from the stormy lullabies
that set the stagy notion
in the park inside the park
tracing loves earthy footpath
the tender animalia
the cozy repeating bits
in hearth and glen
where mother wasn't
lonely stylized forests
did the first cwens
in such water castle
our songs of comfort & praise

Noelle Kocot

Serious the Light

Serious the light on the tiles shining.
Serious the day. Wintering is a streetlamp
Dripping with frost, making a mind neon.
The day drips, too, and we settle in our shoes
Like sailors gazing north. Urban things
Don't hurt us anymore. We are one with the
Tiny lessons brought to us in suitcases.
We are one with the fried exoskeletons of toads.

Bhanu Kapil

The Night I Walked Into The Jungle, I Was Nine Years Old [With: Accompanying Footnotes]

1. Are you nine years old? Yes? No? Firstly, I'm curious. When you wake up in the morning, does your mother, or your grandfather, or your sister, or the person in the bath-robe sipping coffee with fake hazelnut creamer at the kitchen counter…does that person try to make, then ask you to drink (or eat, really, at this point), a banana and turmeric smoothie with whey powder from New Zealand? Secondly, where is New Zealand? If you walked out of your house (which won't work if you live in a third story apartment without a balcony*; don't even try it), which direction would you face? I always know where India is. If the sun is rising, I think, oh, the people in India are washing their faces and getting ready for bed. If night has fallen, I think, okay, they are being forced to eat the smoothie now. If you hadn't noticed, I am Indian. Actually, I'm not. My parents were from India, and I was from where they went to when they left India, and now I am from "here." But you are probably still thinking about the whales and the ocean and the Maoris and all the amazing and difficult and dark blue and glittery things of the Southern Hemisphere, which are hard to face with any precision. Precision is when you are not thinking about the future. My grandfather used to tell me that. He died last year. When I was nine years old, or maybe eight, I can't remember exactly, he said, come on, let's go for a walk. My grandmother called out from the door, wooden spoon in her hand, fresh from stirring a pan of boiled rice, the rice grains gleaming on the wood, *don't be long! Dinner will be ready soon.* And it was.

2. But we didn't come back. Not right then, anyway.

3. I wanted to tell you the story of Hanuman, the famous Monkey King, who slept with his horse each night in the branches of a mango tree. I wanted to tell you the story of how Lord Rama, his wife Sita, and his brother Laxman, were exiled to the jungle for a span of fourteen years, and how Hanuman met them there. It's the story my mother told me, in little bits, every night before I went to sleep. But the more I wrote the story of an adventurous and rather naughty monkey who gave his heart to Rama as soon as he set eyes upon him, the more I wrote myself into the vines and trails of a forest that was real. I started to write a new story, the story of how I walked into the jungle, when I was nine years old. But: which story do **you** want? If the one I am about to tell you does not suit, please write to me immediately and ask for the other one. I will be happy to tell you it in another way, or at least fragments of it, as they come. My e-mail is: thisbhanu@yahoo.com. Get a grown up to write to me, and then I'll write to them, and they can print it out.

3. But back to you. Are you snug? Good. Okay. Here we go. If by any chance you live near Yellowstone Park or the Adirondacks or something, please ignore everything I am about to say. As I said, I was an Indian child, sort of, and what happened next happened in India, in the late afternoon just before you were about to wake up, if you lived in Detroit or Oakland or somewhere else where it rained a lot at certain times of year, which (rain) is conducive to dreams. Conducive means you've relaxed enough to stop being you, entirely. That's something else my grandfather told me, except he said it in Hindi, so I might have got that wrong. Conducive might mean you drink your 8 a.m. curried milkshake, which is bright yellow, which is not even remotely normal, because not even bananas are that color**, even in certain kinds of gum, as a color or flavor, without a fuss.

4. "Don't be late! Don't walk too far! Keep an eye on the time! Dinner's nearly ready! Where are you going? We need some yogurt. Will you pick up some yogurt from the store? Do you have money? Don't forget, we're having okra*** for dinner!" *Yeah, yeah, yeah.*

5. We walked to the edge of town, a small town nestled in the foothills of the Himalayas, called Nangal. There was a river, and an uncle who baked flatbread in the center of town. His hands and face were always covered with soft white flour, and when he hugged you, he smelled of anise. Like red licorice and honey and something else. Shoe polish. I am telling you the story in the past tense, because these are things that happened a long time ago, when I was a child.****

6. And we didn't come back, not that night, not the next morning, and not the lunch-time after that. We returned home the next afternoon. When we walked through the door, my grandmother started shouting, my mom started yelling, and me and my grandfather just looked at each other and smiled. This is the story of that smile.*****

---

*When I was nine years old, I saw a film of Eva Peron on TV. Maybe it wasn't a film. Maybe it was just TV. She was on a balcony with her arms above her in a V. I thought this was exactly how it should be, and decided that when I grew up I would, ideally, live somewhere that had a balcony and that every morning, I'd wake up and drink coffee on it, even though, until I was twenty-two, I thought coffee was completely disgusting. Where do you want to live when you grow up? When I grow up, I want to live in Portugal, by the sea. Wait! I am grown up.

**Ask Hanuman. He'd tell you. If he could speak. Which he does, in the other story.

***Deep fried okra with onions. Enough to make you emigrate to Auckland if you ask me.

****How is that going for you? Childhood. I hope it's going really well. I hope you are happy, and if for any reason you feel sad today, or it's raining out, I hope this story cheers you up, although it does have a really scary and giant black snake in a puddle in it, so, alternatively, I hope this story doesn't make you feel sick. But maybe you are a kid who likes snakes, in which case, please keep reading.***** If you are one of the kinds of kids that hates snakes and starts screaming, even in zoos, you might want to get your friend to read the next part to you while you close your eyes and hum a tune at the same time.

*****My grandfather loved to play chess and he loved roses, so much so that when, at the edge of town, we passed a garden where some rather enormous and fragrant and pink Queen Elizabeth roses were growing, my grandfather knocked on the door of the house. The man who came to the door loved roses too, and soon, we were invited in, and the man's wife brought us little glasses of salty-sweet lemonade while we sat on a little blue sofa. Then it started raining and the man and his wife said we shouldn't leave until it stopped. It stopped, but by that time, my grandfather had noticed the chess set and he and the man played a game, and then another one, and then another. When it was time to go, the man's wife snipped off a long stem and we waved goodbye with the rose, which was very bright, but by that hour, it's light****** was already fading. It was time to go home, but we had lost all sense of time, which happens on the very best of days, and especially if you are walking along the edge of a great forest, which is green, holding a rose, which is pink.

*****My grandfather said: "Let's just go a little further. And then we'll turn back. I'm not hungry yet. Are you?"

******I was wearing a blue and white dress with a print of yellow daisies. I was wearing flip flops. My grandfather was wearing what he always wore – a white shirt and loose white trousers made from cotton. He

was wearing flip-flops too. We walked through the beginning part of the forest*******, where a man with a reddish-gold face was cutting bamboo in a parallel space. He kept popping up as we went deeper in. He had a long knife. "A nomad," said my grandfather, "from Bhutan." The way he said it, he made Bhutan sound a bit like Argentina, a place where any normal person would want to go as soon as they could.

*******It started to rain. And suddenly, it was almost dark. Darkness falls swiftly in the jungle. It (the dark) is made of green sounds and also the sound a river makes, when it is born. The trees rush past you as you walk, and they call out to you and crackle as you step. We stepped into a puddle. We were wearing flip-flops, so we decided to walk straight through. Now, please remember this was a puddle in India, and so it was about the size of a city street, across. Wide. We thought about going around the edge, but we were thinking about the tigers. There are tigers with blue eyes and pink teeth in the jungle. Okay, and this is the snake part, so start humming and stamping your feet if you need to.....NOW. (The next day********, when we got back, and after all the shouting, and my grandmother waving the wooden spoon, and my mother making me drink two "nutritional" milkshakes in a row, we found out that on the FRONT PAGE of the national newspaper, there had been an article about the same exact puddle we had been in. Later that night, a man had been walking through it, just like us, and a great black snake had uncoiled itself from the bottom of the puddle, where it lived, apparently, and had, well, eaten the man. Or something like that. I hope you are not actually nine years old, but maybe seven or fourteen, or thirteen, or some other age, because I was nine when I found that out, and I did not like it at all.)

********How we spent the night: we walked into the jungle and then we slept there. About ten minutes or so after the puddle, which came up to our knees, or my knees, I suppose, we met the man with the knife and the red-gold cheeks, which were burned from the sun. He invited us to his camp, which turned out to be, in a clearing, him, his wife, his brother, his brother's wife, a baby, and maybe another baby too, plus about four goats and six or seven giant, hairy yaks covered with multicolored blankets. I couldn't exactly see, because it was dark, and they'd lit a little fire, but still. It's hard to count babies, or creatures with curly horns (that might not be goats at all when you saw them in daylight, but sheep instead), when you don't want to be rude and stare or anything, what with them being nomads on the level of Eva Peron and probably with houses on a precipice somewhere in a faraway land, which one day a person might be invited to, if they were lucky. Do nomads have homes? All I know is that they were very kind, and let us sleep next to the fire, covered with a furry blanket made of skin. Buffalo skin. And we took the blanket, even though my grandfather was a strict vegetarian, and we drank their tea, which they said was tea, but which had a lot of salt in it, and milky butter. We ate their bread, which was delicious, and that night, I had the most wonderful dreams. I dreamed of a white horse. There was no Hanuman; there was nothing else. There was not even a jungle. The horse appeared in a vast blue space. I told my grandfather the dream when I woke up. He said it was a bad sign. But I didn't think so, and I don't think so now. I think there are animals********* that appear in the night when you are sleeping, and that they keep you safe. Perhaps for you it will be an owl, or a cat, or a dog, or something else.

*********Dear Whoever-you-are (reading this): I hope you walk a long way then come back safe. And when you sleep, whether you have a home or not, I hope you sleep deeply and well, and that the animal, when it comes, does not smell. Though it wouldn't be bad if it did, especially if it was a dog that had just gone for a swim in the sea or something. I am sure that is not a bad smell. Also, write your dreams and adventures down at the end of each day, so that you remember them, when it is your turn to tell someone the story you weren't expecting to tell. There are some other things to discuss, such as monkeys, but I can tell you those stories another time.

Taylor Brady

Words for a Picture of a Bee
—for EH, before she got here—

So there's this world
into which welcome
which we'll come
to call first yours

to give us being
first since new
and now since
now's news of what

you bring into it
being breathing first
into a room
a bit of breathing

room to call as
if a step
or two between
those words we furnish

rooms in a clutter
with until now
breath you breathe
out is outward each

from each in room
to move in
dance where face
your mother worries for

when looking forward looks
aside as glance
called sidelong forward
by what's first yours

to breathe a world
into the words
of world as
news from *over here*

and which is anywhere
we hadn't looked
until the buzz
of breathing out builds

room to breathe in
rhythm face to
face and this
is dancing this is

circling round your newness
and is face
to face which
space makes for us

a face to turn
and find in
turn your face
in breathing out and

in together now words
that call to
turn your face
where looking forward is

a step aside to
step into some
new face to
face you dancing with.

As bee calls bee
in circling *be*
this bee this
being's what you breathe.

CA Conrad

(Soma)tic Poetry Exercise

Soma is an Indo-Iranian ritual drink made from pressing particular psychedelic and energizing plants together. In Vedic and Zoroastrian traditions the drink is identified with the divine. The word Soma is derived from the Sanskrit and Indo-European tongues meaning "to press and be newly born."

Somatic is derived from the Greek, meaning the body. In different medical disciplines it can mean different things, from a cell or tissue, or to the part of the nervous system that controls sensations and movements.

(Soma)tic Poetry works between Soma and Somatic, using any possible THING to study through a variety of experiences for generating notes to generate the poems.

In (Soma)tic Poetry THE FILTERS are words which function as focal points for the information and notes gathered from the exercises. With THE FILTERS you take all of your notes and begin to write poetry about or through these words, shaping and editing as you go. But it's important to note that THE FILTERS are only guides, and to help you shape the poem. Also it's good to use at least 2 FILTER words to prevent the conversation from becoming entirely internal or confessional, meaning that with the extension of extra filters the world-view will broaden and pollinate new ideas as the poem takes shape.

EXERCISE: Shopping Mall Trees
for Eileen Myles

Go to a shopping mall parking lot with trees and other landscaping growing between the cars to create this poem. Find a tree you connect with, feel it out, bark, branches, leaves. Sit on it's roots to see if it wants you OFF! These trees are SICK WITH converting car exhaust and shopper exhale all day! Sit with your tree friend. Don't pay attention to the cars coming in and out of the parking lot, you're here to write poetry, not to worry about what a lunatic you appear to be. Remember what our QUEEN poet of merging celestial bodies Mina Loy said, "If you are very frank with yourself and don't mind how ridiculous anything that comes to you may seem, you will have a chance of capturing the symbol of your direct reaction." Public Space is not easy in shopping mall parking lots, but calmly explain yourself to the security guard like I did when creating this exercise. They will train a camera on you, but the sooner you get rid of them the sooner you can train the camera of your brain. Take notes, feverishly at first. Use a magnifying glass to study the dirt, trunk, to look carefully at leaf veins and bark structure. Notes, take notes, writing quickly, as if you've just discovered a sleeping creature that may wake at any moment and ATTACK YOU! Smell your hand, smell a branch. Study then the sky and buildings and people and everything, every detail. Face one direction and stare for a few seconds. Close your eyes and while they're closed imagine what you saw. Open your eyes and notice what you missed when imagining what you saw. Study what was missed and where and how it exists in relation to your tree friend. Take notes. If you are right-handed then touch the tree with your left hand, for your left hand is the hand which absorbs the world. Then walk to other trees in the parking lot and touch them with your right hand, for your right hand is the hand which sends your messages OUT of you. Touching your right hand to the other trees sends OUT of you the message your tree friend put into you through your left hand. Take notes on what was said from tree to tree. What message were you carrying? Take notes while leaving. Later, at home, close your eyes and remember your tree friend, take more notes from this visit with your memory. Now take all your notes, and using THE FILTERS "TRACT" and "INITIATE," shape your poem.

Anne Waldman

Manatee/Humanity

the manatee is found in shallow slow moving rivers

the manatee moves in estuaries moves in saltwater bays

the manatee in moving moves gently

the manatee is to be found in canals and coastal areas

the manatee is a migratory animal

the manatee is gentle and slow-moving

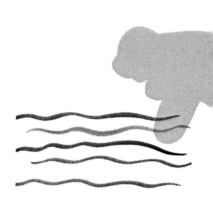

the manatee moves in slow moving rivers slowly

the manatee is completely herbivorous

the West Indian manatee has no natural enemies

the manatee has no natural enemies but unnatural man

the manatee is constantly threatened by man unnaturally

man with his boats and plastic and attitude

the manatee often drowns in canal locks of man

man who makes no concession to manatee

the manatee often dies in flood control structures

man who makes no concession to manatee nor cares of manatee

manatee life manatee fortune

the manatee dies in collision with water craft

man who does not protect the manatee

what steward of the earth is this unnatural man?

man who makes no concession to manatee

the manatee dies with the ingestion of fish hooks

man who unnaturally, makes no concession

the manatee dies from litter and monofilament lines

man who is rank in attitude has no use for manatee

the manatee dies entrapped in crab trap lines

the manatee dies from loss of habitat claimed by man

the manatee is maimed by man, the manatee could be aided by man

man o aid the manatee man come to the manatee heart

a manatee calf is born every 2-5 years

a manatee gestates for a year in the manatee womb

8,400 miles of tidal waters could be for the manatee

11,000 miles of rivers & stream could be for the manatee

10,000 miles of canals would they all be for the manatee

the manatee has more grey matter in the brain than man

the manatee is perhaps thinking archivally deeper than man

ancient days of manatee so many thousands of years

manatee mind, what is the mind of manatee

the manatee has no natural enemies

the manatee is completely herbivorous

the metabolism of the manatee is slow, moves slowly

the manatee moves in estuaries, moves in saltwater bays

the manatee moves in slow moving rivers the manatee is gentle

the manatee offspring nurses for up to 2 years

the manatee learns everything from the manatee mother

the manatee mothers and offspring sing to one another

the manatee have large ear-bones

chirps whistles squeaks of the manatee

the manatee in moving slowly moves gently

oscillations of the manatee moving between the manatee ears

ears of the manatee mother and manatee offspring

manatee are our sirenians, and live in the house of the sirens

where are the human sanctuaries for the manatee

manatees mermaids sirens singing move slowing

the manatee mother and calf so bonded

female manatee bonded with her just one manatee offspring

Sarah Anne Cox

The Carpet Square

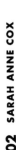

A Play for 3 or 20

Characters:
Ben, a boy who does not attend school
Tom, a boy, Ben's friend, who does attend school
Teacher, a person, an adult
Mother, a woman
Other students, at least 3 but as many as 20. None have speaking parts, so you may add or subtract as many students as you like.

In front of a closed curtain, a mother and son walk back and forth across the stage as if they are taking a long walk.

Mom: Ok you wanted to see what school was and we're almost there. I think we turn right here and walk down this street and we'll hit Edith Sitstill Elementary.

Ben: Great, are you going to come too?

Mother: No. Moms aren't allowed in school. It's only for children. The teacher said it would be best if I didn't come in and left you at the door.

Ben: Really? How weird.

Mother: I think she's worried I'll hover…*(Worried)* You don't have to go.

Ben: No, I want to see it. It sounds fun! No parents! Maybe I'll like it.

Mother: Ok then, here we are. *(Stops in middle of stage and waves her hand as if to show something.)* I'll see you at three. Be good. I love you. *(Gives him a kiss on the cheek.)* Look for Tommy. He said he would help you get the hang of things.

(The curtain opens. The stage is bare. There are 20 children of various ages running in chaotic circles. They each hold in their hand ribbon sticks from rhythmic gymnastics. The ribbons make zigzags and circles and fly through the air. No one looks at the ribbons. There is music, county fair type, playing. Something like the Gilberto Gil's, Domingo no Parque.)

Ben: Bye Mom. *(Walks away without looking back.)*

Tom: Hi Ben. Are you ready for school?

Ben: Hi Tom. Yes I think so. This looks so fun! *(Begins to run and mimic the crowd.*
All of a sudden, a very loud bell or buzzer goes off and the children stop, spin the ribbon in circles above their heads and drop to the floor.)

Ben: (Alarmed) OH MY GOD. What happened? What are they doing?

Tom: Oh, playtime is over, and school is starting. That's what you do when you hear the bell ring.

(The children then get up and start lining up on the stage. There are maybe four lines, depending on the number of children. The children wait.)

Ben: What are they doing now? It's looks like they're going to build something…Maybe they will build a pyramid…No they are building a snake. *(He watches the children file out.)*

Tom: No, they aren't building a snake.

Ben: Sure they are. Look at it hiss and curve. …You know, they need summore zigzags in their snake, yeah more snakey. *(He begins to slither.)*

Tom: No, they aren't trying to be a snake. They are trying to be in line. Come on let's go.
(Tugs at Ben's sleeve.)

Ben: Why would they do that? That's dull. Why wouldn't they be snakes instead?

Tom: Because we need to be organized, standing in a straight line, to go into the classroom. Come on.

Ben: Ok, but I am a snake. *(Slithers into the last line.)* Um Tom? *(He says while snaking around.)* Why do we need to be organized?

Tom: *(Walking ahead of him.)* Dunno Ben. You always have to walk in lines at school.

Ben: Always?

Tom: Yeah, ever since kindergarten. We had to learn how to walk in a line. Now we line up to go out, line up to go in, line up to go down the hall, line up to go up stairs, line up to have lunch, line up to kick the ball…

Ben: Yeah?

Tom: Of course! It's one of the things you learn at school. *(He speaks with certainty.)*

(They walk off stage and back on, still in line.)

Tom: Ben?

Ben: Yeah?

Tom: Maybe it's because there are so many of us.

(The boys arrive in the classroom. There are many small bare desks and one large one with many things on it: a pencil sharpener, scissors, markers, pencils, tape, stickers, stapler, etc.)

Tom: Ok. Here we are; you sit there, and I sit here.

(Ben eyes the room sees the desk with the teacher's chair.)

Ben: I want to sit there. *(He points to the large desk.)*

Tom: *(sighing)* This is going to be a long day. You can't sit there, Ben.

Ben: But that's the big desk. I mean look at it—and it has scissors…and tape…and all those pens…

Tom: The Teacher sits there, Ben, The Teacher.

Ben: I think we should take turns sitting at the big desk. Oh, yoo hoo, *(he says waving)*.

Teacher: Why you must be Ben. I'm very pleased to meet you. *(Holds out hand for shaking.)* Now go sit down over there.

Ben: I would like to sit in the big desk.

Teacher: Well, that's where I sit.

Ben: I think we should take turns sitting at the big desk.

Teacher: Ben, this is the teacher's desk, so I need to sit in it. Tom can you show Ben his desk?

(Tom shows Ben the little desk.)

Teacher: Ok, to the carpet everyone. *(Claps twice.)* Tom will you please show Ben where the carpet squares are?

(Tom leads Ben to a tall stack of carpet squares piled high. All the children grab the squares and begin to sit down in front of the teacher, who is still writing something at her desk.)

Tom: Yeah, ok. So here are the squares, and everyone gets one.

Ben: Wow that's cool, what does it do? I think mine can fly. *(Throws carpet square on the floor and begins to ride it, balancing.)* I have a magic carpet…I'm flying to New Zealand, watch out. No, follow me. We'll go together, Tom.

Tom: Um Ben….um Ben?

Ben: Whoa, look at me. Maybe I can surf it. Or it's my skateboard. *(Tries to ollie several times.)* Whoa, check it out. Let's hit the pipe!

Tom: You are meant to sit on it.

Ben: What? I can't hear you. I'm getting tubed. *(Crouches down on his square.)*

Tom: I said, IT'S FOR SITTING ON!

Ben: OK. OK. Sitting on it. Like a magic carpet?

Tom: No, sitting on it and looking at the teacher. See, you sit on your carpet and pay attention. And maybe the teacher calls on you. Maybe she doesn't, but you have to stay on your square. And you can't move over and touch anybody else's square OR the area around their square OR their bodies. You have to stay in your own space.

Ben: *(Ben stares at Tom for a moment.)* Huh. Bummer.

Teacher: Ok, let's all sit down, hands to yourself, stay on your squares. Very good, class. Now let's do some math problems together on this white board I have here...seven minus seven...

(Stage goes dark and then light again. They are still on the carpet and most of the children are holding their heads up with their hands, some are spacing out, staring at the floor or playing with their shoes. Suddenly the loud buzzer goes off again.)

Ben: *(jumps awake)* OH MY GOD it's that buzzer again! What is going on?

Tom: Oh no, that's the good buzzer. It means it's time for lunch. Lunch and recess. You'll like recess Ben. You can do whatever you want. Oh, except there's something you'll need to know. *(They start to line up.)* Recess and lunch are combined so if you stay too long at lunch, you get less time at recess.

Ben: Oh, but I'm hungry.

Tom: Yeah, me too. But eat real fast, so you can play outside.

Ben: But don't we have all afternoon?

Tom: No, we have 30 minutes! Twenty minutes for lunch and ten minutes for recess. That's why some of us guys don't eat our lunch at all. Maybe we'll have a bite, but we'd rather go out and play. You'll see. That 30minutes goes by quick.

Ben: Ok, I'll try to eat fast. But you're making my stomach ache.

Tom: Sorry, there just isn't time. Recess is the best part of the day. You don't want to miss it.

(Lights dim as the boys depart. We hear a series of Bells/Buzzers. The lights come up, and the class comes back on stage in a line. They sit at desks.)

Ben: That was too short.

Tom: You're telling me.

Ben: I'm tired. I want to go home.

Tom: We're almost done.

Teacher: I'm going to pass out your homework sheets. Everyone pull out your homework folder. *(The teacher begins to pass out worksheets. It seems never ending. She keeps passing out more and more sheets.)*

Ben: How many of these are there?

Tom: Five, no six, no seven. *(Recounts them again. Smiles.)* Yes, seven.

Ben: *(Looking at each of the sheets in disbelief.)* But didn't we do this all day? Why do we have to do it at home?

Tom: *(sighs)* I dunno Ben. Maybe we didn't do enough of it.

Ben: This is going to take forever.

Tom: You'll get the hang of it.

Ben: No, (*still looking at the worksheets then straight at Tom*) no. I don't think I will.

Tom: What you mean? You're not going to do homework? Come on, you have to. If you don't do your homework, they take away your recess. You can't win.

Ben: No, I mean I don't think this is for me, this whole school thing, the lines, the desks, the sitting, the carpet squares. I don't want that.

Tom: (*offhandedly*) Yeah, but everybody has to go to school.

Ben: No, Tom, they don't. We don't. And I'm not going to.

Tom: Are you just going to quit?

Ben: Yeah. This just isn't for me.

Tom: But don't you just do the same stuff at home, at "homeschool"?

Ben: Some do, some don't, everyone's different. But it's not like this. This is not for me. No school is so much more fun. It's learning all the time. You get to ask questions about whatever you want to know.

Tom: Yeah…

Ben: Yeah. (*Turning to the class.*) Come on, quit with me! We'll all quit. They can't stop us.

Tom: But Ben, I kind of like worksheets…

Ben: That's ok; my sister loves worksheets, I hate them. It's like I said, we are all different. We shouldn't ALL do the same thing at the same time.

Lights dim and curtain.

Production Notes

The Teacher might easily play the role of the Mother. I like this idea because it would enact the artificial separation between these roles. We think they are two different jobs, but in the early years are they? One of the best compliments my son ever gave to a teacher was that she was like a mom.

This play can involve as many people as want to take part. The role of Tom can be split up between many people, each taking a certain task such as the line, desk, carpet square, et cetera. The whole class could be involved in explaining school to Ben. Furthermore, the gender of the characters is a bit arbitrary. Ben and Tom could easily become Bonnie and Tamara.

Finally, I think the adults should play the children's parts and vice versa. We tend to accept that school is a frightfully boring, rigid but necessary evil. So often what we accept in children's lives is something that we would never dream of accepting in our own. I think it might be far more entertaining and enlightening to have the adults act out the scenes that our children are so often subjected to.

Julie Patton

Bee My Guest

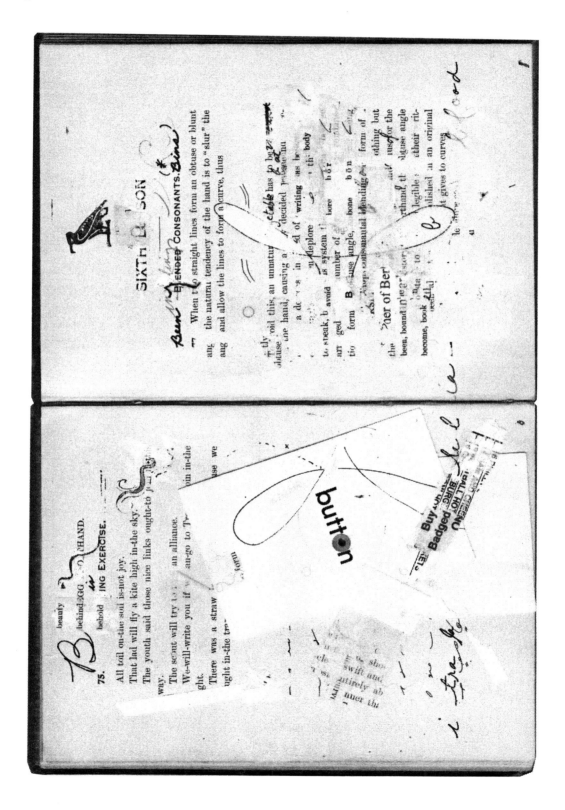

Parts of this piece, the button, for example, were
originally colored in. Please draw on these pages as you see fit.

Kaia Sand

song from a beached music box

for Jessi

when I wear a dream coat
long with crumpled velvet
I'll umbrella you in the rain
warm you in the snow
and spread it on the sand when we picnic
in the ocean's neighborhood

near some small diner
where we'll seat some friends
we'll turn the booths to houses
hang lanterns from their doors

on one low blue table
we might try to grow some food
let's water with teacups, till with forks
and our food will feed the neighborhood

to our buttoned cuffs
we might pin straw and bendy flowers
that we'll name seven names
from an alphabet of Xs

when I have a chessboard to set in front of you
our queens will meet and delight each other
and they'll forget to play

when we hear three rainbows
sing like fifteen radios
when you ride a bike
with wheels that spin like suns
when you clap as fast
as flapping hummingbird wings

colors will croon for hours
in the flaming amber and its leaves

when you chat with mice
who animate the yard
you'll remind the sunflowers
to droop down their heads
so seeds and secrets fall

maybe we'll find a phone
on which to place a call
let's ring the trees next door
and tell them their shade is good

and let's stage a government
like a daily birthday party
where promises will be primroses
that wilt if they just aren't true

if we find five stop signs
to prop at any corners
we'll perimeter the Pentagon
mixing memos into songs

let's weave the bus lines
routed through our city
into woolen blankets
to warm the coldest slumber

and let's build a music box
to crank power for the city
to breach the dams and loose the salmon
and thank candles for their burning

thank candles for their burning
in this world of our making

let's make a world like that
as promising as primroses
blooming bright as hummingbirds
let's make a world like that

Rosmarie Waldrop

APRICOT MADNESS

A Song for Christopher Montgomery

My head may be a cabbage
my heart an artichoke
my face a mouldy kumquat
my left eye a bulging yoke

my mouth is badly paved
but I laugh like twenty whales
I wag my red rattle rag
and flutter my eyelid scales

and sing
and sing
and sing
in my apricot madness

My shoulders my droop like a bottle
my ears may be upside down
my breasts like tobacco pouches
my egg getting bald on the crown

my nose may be a coatrack
my drumsticks my be like wire
my feet damp as the evening
but my armpits smell like fire

as I dance
as I dance
as I dance
in my apricot madness

I may have lost my compass
I've trichinosis in my ham
but there's method in my apricot
and madness in my jam

my sap is turning to resin
my bread may be going stale
I may have rusty guts
but one thing's hearty and hale

and that's
and that's
and that's
my apricot madness

I'm turning into a gargoyle
getting drunk on rain
but the moon is no cold pineapple
as long as I got my brain

in its apricot madness

Harryette Mullen

Wipe That Simile Off Your Aphasia

as horses as for
as purple as we go
as heartbeat as if
as silverware as it were
as onion as I can
as cherries as feared
as combustion as want
as dog collar as expected
as oboes as anyone
as umbrella as catch can
as penmanship as it gets
as narcosis as could be
as hit parade as all that
as icebox as far as I know
as fax machine as one can imagine
as cyclones as hoped
as dictionary as you like
as shadow as promised
as drinking fountain as well
as grassfire as myself
as mirror as is
as never as this

Eileen Myles

Jacaranda

What's
the feminine
of feet
I didn't
know I
could
have
a lavender
tree

Maria Damon

For Selma Damon

A few years ago, when I asked my mother what she wanted for Christmas, she said all she wanted was respect. She got this (instead), but took it in stride. I stitched in bright red cotton on a white linen background; those are Danish national colors (she's Danish, and came to the US right after World War II when she was thirty years old). The heart and crown are also typical Danish motifs. I learned to cross-stitch when I was about 8, in Denmark, from my mother's sister and other older female relatives.

Kristin Palm

I Traded This Poem for a Handmade Bag
(for Nicole)

There is a lake

There is a lake and there are fish

There is a lake and there are fish and there is a girl who paints the fish

There are colors

There are colors she uses to paint the fish

And shapes

There are shapes of the fish

The girl is not a fish and she knows this

None of us are fish no matter how much we like to swim

And you cannot swim in this lake

Not if you are human

If you are a cormorant

You can swim in the lake

You can swim in the lake

And because you have the ability to wet your wings

You can dive deep for fish

And you can swallow them using your long, narrow throat

Then you can return to the surface

And raise your regal head

And if you are a black-crowned night heron

You can forage for bugs along the water's edge

After dark

And if you are a water rat

You can swim all the way from the rocks out to the island

These are the fish I know:

> pipefish
>
> surgeonfish
>
> tonguefish
>
> jawfish
>
> damselfish

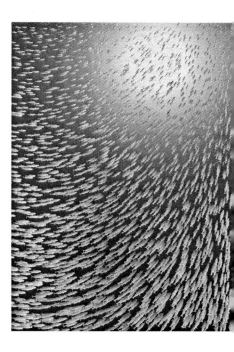

Nicole, we are not fish

And the lake is not real

I mean, nature did not put it there

Some men constructed it

Using concrete and water diverted

From the bay

They built the islands, too

Where I sit and watch the birds

The fish they catch are not the same

As the fish you paint

The fish they catch are:

       sculpins

       smelt

       yellow-tailed gobies

       striped bass

       minnows

You tell me you tried to paint real fish

The kind of fish a bird might catch

But you like so much better the ones you see

In your head

Me, I could never paint fish

Not the ones in the water

Or the ones in my mind

I can only tell you

their names

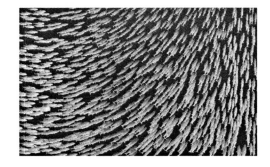

Julien Poirier

MOON LION

There's a lion on the moon
and when you pour moonlight over the lion
the moon turns the color of lion tea

Did you know this?
the moon lion is lonely
so lonely she has grown very smart

It's as if the tropical flowers
that crowd the glowing white rock
were really tropical flowers
like something you would find
in the Caribbean; in fact they are
cool (but not "cold") touching them
is like washing your hands
in a silent film

Back to the lion.
Watch her blink

Do you see how the whites of her eyes
must have been painted by whoever
painted the moon? how close
the stars seem to be to each other!
as a French poet (whose name
I never knew) once said

"They nod over the hedge
like farmers with their caps
in their hands"

The lion is touched by their profusion
touched by the statue
of a waterfall

POEM

Morning moon—
My toothpick's wrong way round.

Jaime Cortez

The Jesus Donut

Soon as the van turned off San Juan Street onto our dirt road, you could see the cloud of dust chasing it. Didn't look like nothing special at first. Just a white van turning into a brown van. When it got closer, we saw it said "Dough Re Mi," on the side, and I wondered what it was about. The driver opened the door and stepped out. With his pink face, white shirt, white hair and little mustache, he kind of looked like Mister Kentucky Fried Chicken. But he wasn't selling no chicken. No. It was way better than any old chicken. He stopped the van right by where me and Cesar were playing *changalalai*. He went to the back of the van and opened up the two doors. Of course we were wondering what he was doing. Usually The Boss is the only white that ever comes to the camp, so it's not like we get to see real Americans here every day. He looked at us, then made a little hook with his finger and called us with it. I pointed to myself, like I was saying "me?" He nods his head "yes." Then the girls stop playing hopscotch and come over too. The five of us all stood around him and he had a big ol' smile, like he was gonna tell us the greatest secret ever.

"Hablan Español?" he asked. Everyone was real quiet and surprised. It was like when I saw a parrot say "Lucy I'm Hooooome" at my *tias* house, we didn't think he could do that. Then Carlos answered.

"Yeah, we can speak Spanish." Cesar was so brave, just talking to that big pink gringo with the white hair just like that.

"*Muy bueno*. That is very good," he said real slow, like he thought we couldn't understand.

Then he turned and opened up the two doors of the back of the van. Inside, it had silver metal drawers one on top of the other. He grabbed the handle of the bottom drawer and opened it, and everyone went "waaaauuuw," "holy guacamole," and "no way, Jose!" The whole drawer was fulled up with Donuts! Shiny perfect donuts all in a row like little tan soldiers. The smell was really, really nice. So we all just stood there and he smiled at us and we smiled at him. Then he opened the next drawer and it was all chocolate donuts and some of them had little rainbow sprinkles on them, or even better, coconut. And this drawer was so beautiful nobody said nothing. It was like a magic show. He was smiling so hard his eyes got tiny like the cooks at the Chopstick restaurant. Then he opened the top drawer and it was hundred percent cookies. Huge cookies bigger than your hand. Some had chocolate chips and some were shaped like smiley faces with yellow stuff. For a long time, we just stood and looked and tried to believe it that someone bought a whole vanfull of donuts to the Wyrick Ranch homes, where nobody ever comes unless they're workers or family.

"Can I have one?" said Little Lola.

"No stupid," said my sister Sylvie. "They're not free. You have to pay."

"How much I gotta pay?"

"Not too much," said the old man. "They're twelve cents each or two for twenty cents."

"Oh."

Then everyone got real quiet and kind of embarrassed. I didn't have twelve cents or even one cents. We didn't have no money to buy no shiny donuts. We all just stand there, all quiet, and his face gets even more pinker. Then he finally says, "Well, maybe next time you can buy a donut." He closes the cookie drawer, then the beautiful chocolate drawer and then Olga says,

"Wait. Please can I please have two donuts?"

"Of course you can, little lady. What kind of donuts would you like?" Everyone's staring at Olga, cuz where did she get money? He opens the drawers like steps, so we can see the three at the same time. He gets a little pink and white bag and a little piece of paper and he smiles. Olga smiles too and she points to a chocolate donut with sprinkles. He puts it in the bag. Then she points to the shiny glazed donuts on the bottom drawer. He puts that in the bag.

"Twenty cents," he says.

Everybody stops breathing. What's she gonna do? She gonna take the bag and run? That would be stupid, cuz he could chase her in the van, besides, if she did that, Grandma would hit her so hard, she'd see the Devil through a hole. I don't know what that means, but grandma always says that and it sounds pretty serious.

Olga bends down and unties her tennies. She takes it off her foot and there, in the bottom of the stinky rotten tennie shoe is a perfect, shiny quarter! She picks it up and gives it to him. His face gets red again, and he puts the quarter into his change machine on his belt. He pops out a nickel and gives it to her.

"Thank you, darling," he says.

"Thank you," she says.

"Anyone else?" he asks. No one says yes. No one says no. So he smiles and closes up the drawers, shuts the doors and gets into the car. He drives away slowly, waves at us one time and then goes faster down the road. We all stand looking at Olga.

"Where'd you get that money?"

"My papi gave me gave me two quarters for my domingo cuz I helped out in the house.

"They PAY YOU to help in the house?" asked Sylvie. Olga just smiled.

"What you gonna do with that extra donut?" asks Lola.

"It's not an *extra* donut, bonehead!" said Cesar. "You know what she's gonna do? She's gonna scarf them up - both of them." His voice sounded like something that got dropped and cracked.

"I'm just asking, that's all," said Lola. You can tell she wants to cry. I don't blame her.

"You guys want some donut?" says Olga. Whoa.

"Really?" I ask.

"Yeah." Nobody can believe it that she's gonna let us have some of those beautiful fancy donuts.

"Heck Yeah we do!" says Cesar.

"You can have some," she says, "but you have to do what I say, and you can't taste the chocolate one."

"Well what do we have to do?" asks Sylvie.

"First you have to wash your hands and your faces and fix your hair, like on Sunday."

"What for?" asked Sylvie.

"I don't have to tell you what for. If you want donut, you just do it," she said. So we go into the shower room. Two of us get on each of the sinks and we start washing. We use the big brown Mexican soap to wash our faces. We wet our hair and push it back down with our hands. We dry our hands on our pants and come back out.

"Now you have to get in a line on your knees," said Olga. Cesar's forehead gets all red. Here it comes -

"This is STOOPID!" he shouts.

"If you don't like it, go away then. But if you want donut, do what I say."

Cesar's all quiet and then he gets in line on his knees. One by one we all do the same. Olga goes to the first one in line. It's Sylvie. She cuts off a little piece of donut between her two fingers, holds it next to Sylvie's mouth and says, "Body of Christ."

Sylvie says, "Amen."

"STOP!" says Cesar. "This is stupid. First of all, girls can't be no priests. Second of all, you can't pretend that's a host. That's blasphemy!" Olga puts the little piece of donut on Sylvie's tongue. Sylvie closes her mouth and she just kneels there, really quiet, with a little smile on her face. Cesar points his finger at Olga's face and shouts, "I'm not gonna do blasphemy for some donut! C'mon Mauricio," he says to me, "let's get outta here." He walks away and in a few steps he turns back and sees me on my knees.

"Are you coming, Mauricio?" he asks.

"I will. As soon as I get some donut." He looks at me. Now his ears are red too.

"If you stay here, you can't hang around with me no more." This is serious. I wanna follow him fifty percent, but I want donut like 90 percent, so I stay.

Olga goes down the line and gives everyone some Jesus Donut. I am the second to the last, and I keep watching the donut get smaller and smaller. I should have gotten in the front of the line, then I wouldn't have to be kneeling in the dirt, afraid the donut will finish before it comes to me. But the donut doesn't disappear, and when she gets to me, there's lots left. She cuts off a little piece for me.

"Body of Christ."

"Amen," I say, and I open my mouth. She puts the piece of donut on my tongue. I close my mouth. I close my eyes.

This is the way Jesus should taste. Like a sweet cloud that gets tinier and tinier in your mouth, and then it's just a memory that lives inside of you.

The last piece of donut, the biggest piece, she eats herself. She chews and chews like a little cow, then she finishes. She opens her hands up like two wings, and says,

"You may go in peace, this mass is over."

She walks away, swinging her pink and white bag. We get up, and clean our knees. She gets to her house, and pulls open the screen door with the big holes a full-grown goat could walk into, and then she goes inside. Soon as she gets into the house, everyone starts talking. Everybody has some big opinion about Olga and the Jesus Donut.

"That was good."

"That was weird."

"She's crazy."

"She's nice, she gave me donut, so I don't care what she did."

"That really was blasphemy. We should have beat her up, then took the donut."

"Right in front of us, she ate half of it herself."

"She made us get in the dirt and wash our faces for one little tiny crumb." "Nobody forced you, so stop complaining. Besides, it was dee-licious!"

The more I think about it, the more I hate her and her donut. The way she pretended she was a priest. Cesar was right. Girl's can't be priests anyways, so no way can she do communion. Olga comes back out of her house.

When she gets close enough to hear, we stop talking about her.

"'Church will be tomorrow at 12 in the afternoon in my kitchen," she says.

"You're gonna let us have the Chocolate donut?" asks Lola.

"Yup. Body of Christ at 12 o'clock," she says.

"Right on, sister!" says Sylvie. Wow. She's gonna give us a taste of the chocolate. This is getting really good!

That night when I go to sleep, I don't really go to sleep. I go to worry. I keep thinking about that Chocolate donut. If the glazed donut tasted like Jesus, what does the chocolate donut with sprinkles taste like? The more I think about it, the more madder I get. If the chocolate donut is even better, how can we just stand around watching her eating with so much donut in her trap she can't even close it while we only get one little taste? Its not fair, but all I can do now is wait and have my donut crumb like everyone else.

The next morning, nobody says nothing about it. I help my dad wash the car, vacuum the car, then wax the car. I hate waxing. He gets so mad. "Do it harder! Do it faster! Don't let the wax dry *muchacho*, what's wrong with you?!" What's wrong is I hate waxing your car. You want it so perfect, you do it! That's what I would say but I don't want to get smacked on the head, so I just keep on waxing. When I get my own car, I'm never gonna wax no matter what. At 11:38, we finish. He says go wash up for lunch. I say okay, but instead I go and wait in front of Olga's house to wait for church. In a little while, Sylvie and Lola come. Their faces are washed and their hair is all shiny. Olga comes out.

"You can enter now, brothers and sisters," she says. We open the door and go into the kitchen.

"Please kneel," she says. We get onto our knees like before.

"For what we are about to receive," she says. "Let us be truly thankful," we say. She goes to the cupboard, and opens it. She moves a little sack of flour and a can of Spaghettios. She pulls out a little plate and then she says "Oh no!" real soft, then she shouts "oh NO!"

The donut is covered with black ants! Hundreds of them. Theres so many of them the donut looks like it's wearing a black sweater. We all say "Ewwwww!" and "Gross, man!" and the ants crawl off the plate and up her arm, and Lola screams and Olga squishes the ants on her arm. She takes the donut to the sink, and hits it against the side to knock the ants off, but they just keep crawling up her arm. Then we really start laughing and capping on her.

"Hah hah! You shoulda ate the donut when you had a chance, bonehead!"

"Yeah Olga, you can take your donut and stick it up your butt!"

"We told you it was blasphemy, now look what happened."

She turns on the water, and puts the donut under it, and tries to clean it, and of course, it breaks into pieces with wet, drowned ants all over it like sprinkles!

"You can't wash a donut, retard!" I say, and we all start laughing for reals now. Olga starts to cry and tries to kill the ants on her arm and her shirt. The more she cries, the more we laugh, till finally she shouts, "Get out!" and she grabs a broom and swings it like a mom, and smacks me in the shoulder, but I don't care, cuz I'm laughing so good. We run outta the house like rabbits and we can't stop laughing because Olga's mass is finished, and now we can laugh to the sky, because laughing about the drowned donut with the sweater of ants is even better than eating it!

Danna Lomax &
Dana Teen Lomax

FOr Middle SchOOlers & Other Maligned Citizens

HOrmOne gift in black with ear buds and a cap

HOrmOne gift Of laugh laugh laugh like there's nO tOmOrrOw

The scratch & sniff Of the hOrmOne gift

The hOrmOne makes see-thrOugh Of everything gift

The gift Of I'm nOt sure why I'm hOrmOne yelling at my parents right nOw

"He hOrmOne said that she hOrmOne said that he" gift

hey bff! OMG luv dat hOrmOne lol gift ttyl

HOrmOne bOuncing me Off Of yOu gift

HOrmOne gift mOre curiOus than ready

Find Out whO I am by trying tO be like everyOne else hOrmOne gift

HOrmOne gift Of stay up waaaay late and sleep with eyes Open in Math

Transparent gift cOcOOn of hOrmOne apple breasts beard hair and hips emergent

HOrmOne try On snOtty try On sarcastic try On pretty bOy/girl etc. gift

Underneath spark Of sOft warm snuggle hug hOrmOne gift

Gift Of that's nOt fair hOrmOne seeking justice

Rosamond S. King

Experimints in Spellchick

If you interrogate what hippens in the psat, you well bee able to predick the futour.
Her genus lies in the fat that her writing perfectually invects the reeder in. [sic! dangling preparation]
Are you cop-dependent? Take these supple testes and keep track of your scare.
It is rediculous to right this as prose. But the assay is paid more than the verso.
If it
snot a prose
poom is
it less
xprinti-mental
a avent guard
in no votive end
market able?
Dint be two heard in the yolks in charge. They ear gist weeping the fits of their Labradors.

Three Poems

    freshshsh squeeeezzed
    ohrange juissssce
    eeeeeat ssmuuuuth ferrawth
    on top sso much
    ehfort for sssuch a likkle glass

There is no heat in the hot.
It ran for
a long time, but was
only lukewarm.

Roll the curlers under. That
will keep them close to the
scalp. Curlicue, curly yew.
Scalped. Close to and don't
brush, just run your fingers
through.

Nicole Brodsky

I Looked Fine When I Left the House

You started out looking gentle today in brown braids pinned around each side of your head.

In the mirror.

I love me.

The grace of my bangs smoothed out of her eyes and the small hairs escaped from their plaits hum around my temples, a halo.

Then it rained, and, well, you know you'll hate it later.

Frizzy around my face with nothing to smooth me, every hair gone hazy.

You can't stop being good because the weather turned.

But I can whisper in my mirror: Love, when it comes to your hair, I disagree.

Christian Bök

THE DOOMSDAY SONG

(FOR FRIEDRICH NIETZSCHE—UPON THE DEATH OF SUPERMAN)

1. KROOM! KROOM! KRAKOOM!
   KRAKA-DOOM! KA-DOOM!

2. FLOOM
   FWOOM BOOM

3. KRAKADOOM BUDDADOOM

4. CHOOM
   KA-CHOOM KA-DOOM SHOOM!

5. KTOOM
   KTOOM!
   BUH-BOOM! BUH-BOOM!
   PTOOM!
   KRAKATOOM! THOOM!

6. BA-DOOM!
   BA-DOOM BRA-DOOM! THOOM!

7. (APPENDIX)

BLAM BAM BKAM
BRAM DRAM
DBAM
KRAK KDAM

Wanda Coleman

COFFEE

steam rises over my nose

against this night

cold empty room as wide as my throat; eases/flows

river a mocha memory from Aunt Ora's

kitchen. she made it in the

big tin percolator and poured the brew into thick

white fist-sized mugs and

put lots of sugar and milk in it for me and

the other kids who loved it better than chocolate

and the neighbor woman used to tell her and us

wasn't good for young colored children

to drink. it made you get blacker

and blacker

Rachel Zolf

done

Erin Wilson

I set off to sail

before launching, I stopped to look carefully
at those small dry plants that grow best in the wind
tiny flowers in the pale colors of the seaside
the colors of rocks, sandy soil, the sky

I plucked a leaf between my fingers
I don't pretend to know its name
or to be interested in its history
I just wanted to smell it
to know
how it captured the sea into chlorophyll,
turned sea air into something I could feel on my skin, could smell

I was at sea
long enough to get the hang of the water
to figure out
how to use my slingshot to kill the gulls who tried to feast on my hair
long enough to drink the rainwater collected in my canvas hat
to weave a blanket of seaweed, a dark green protection for sleeping

other things happened too
clouds rushed past my boat
trailing white thoughts that told me
to reach my hands into the waves
split the moon into two slivers
the white of a clear night

one morning I woke on the shore
I still don't understand how I got as far as I did
from Peoria to Richmond, from San Francisco to Miami.
He said,
It is bottomlessness that worries me
I said,
That's what worries me too

Joan Larkin

IF YOU WERE GOING TO GET A PET

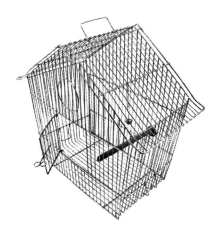

If you were going to get a pet,
what kind of animal would you get.
—Robert Creeley

CHARACTERS
Child
Parent

PLACE
A moving train

TIME
Winter

The light outside grows darker, colder, as dusk comes on.

CHILD
Tell me again.

PARENT
We were poor and hungry.

CHILD
But you had Black Dog. Black Dog was smart. Fearless. Loyal.

PARENT
The house was old.

CHILD
Made of stone.

PARENT
The damp and cold went into our bones. There were deep cracks in the stone walls.
The windows shook in the wind,

CHILD
and Black Dog barked.

PARENT
Howled.

CHILD
You were hungry.

PARENT
We missed our mothers,

CHILD
especially at night.

PARENT
We cried.

CHILD
Howled.

PARENT
In daylight we looked for food. There were still turnips to dig out of the garden.

CHILD
I hate the taste of turnips.

PARENT
Some kale still grew, even in the cold.

CHILD
What's kale?

PARENT
A tough, scratchy leaf—

CHILD
(finishing the sentence)
—that's good for you!

PARENT
We searched under the trees for mushrooms. We had a little bread—

CHILD
and that's why the rats came.

PARENT
There were rats in the old house. They came where we slept.
They came for the bread we took into bed with us.

CHILD
And didn't Black Dog chase the rats, and eat them?

PARENT
We fed Black Dog our food. We waited quietly for the rats to leave. We didn't want to frighten them.

CHILD
Black Dog grew fat.

PARENT
Black Dog devoured any crumb that fell.

CHILD
You were waiting for your mothers to come.

PARENT
They sent letters on thin blue paper. My mother wrote to me—

CHILD
"Be good!"

PARENT
"Be like the others."

CHILD
"Take care of Black Dog."

PARENT
We practiced running and took cold baths. We copied formulas, improved our accents.

CHILD
"Be like the others!"

PARENT
We kept diaries. A boy kissed me as we stood under a tree together, holding hands.

CHILD
Everywhere you went, Black Dog came with you.

PARENT
School room, turnip patch, woods.

CHILD
Black Dog, Black Dog!

PARENT
His eyes watched us. His soft coat grew coarse in the winter cold.

CHILD
Black Dog was keeping you safe.

PARENT
We had no more bread. Black Dog hunted rats in the night,

CHILD
and ate them!

PARENT
Black Dog growled in the doorway—a low growl in the throat that rose higher and became a wolf's howl.

(CHILD growls, barks, howls.)

PARENT
We would try to sleep—

CHILD
but Black Dog—

PARENT
waiting for that terrible barking we knew would wake us.

CHILD
And Black Dog's eyes—

PARENT
Black Dog's eyes burned like coals in the night.

CHILD
And you stopped sleeping.

PARENT
Asleep, we dreamed Black Dog. Awake, we watched over our shoulders.

CHILD
You watched for Black Dog.

PARENT
Black Dog could smell us.

CHILD
Followed you.

PARENT
Wherever we went.

CHILD
You ran to the woods.

PARENT
When Black Dog was sleeping.

CHILD
Black Dog was dreaming you'd left him.

PARENT
We ran deep into the woods, far from the stone house.

CHILD
You couldn't bring anything with you.

PARENT
We were trying to get to the mountain and then—

CHILD
Black Dog couldn't find you!

PARENT
We crossed a stream—

CHILD
You drank the water.

PARENT
We drank the icy water as we waded across on slippery stones.

CHILD
Holding hands. Trying not to fall.

PARENT
We reached the mountain and climbed in the dark.

CHILD
All of you?

PARENT
Some of us reached the mountain.

CHILD
Black Dog followed as far as the stream.

PARENT
We always knew Black Dog could find us.

CHILD
Black Dog! Black Dog!

PARENT
It's night now. Time for sleeping.

CHILD
Black Dog watches me all night.

PARENT
Black Dog—

CHILD
—still lives in the house.

PARENT
Close your eyes.

CHILD
I think I can hear Black Dog breathing.

PARENT
Black Dog is sleeping now.

CHILD
I think I see him moving.

PARENT
Stirring in his sleep.

CHILD
Black Dog.

PARENT
Stirring in his sleep.

(Lights dim to darkness as the train continues on its long way.)

Marthe Reed

Canon: a strange loop

a red & gold box
the fretted lid of a box
a line of black moves as a cresting wave
etched & ornately carved
shadow

a red cloth
a cloth stamped in white
a red box
a box which is a basket & no cloth

a handful of black seeds
copper coins in a box
a ceramic box
a rectangular bowl

a sixth box
a box as a mask
leering eyes & tusks
jut from its sides a perilous box

a first box
a box among many
memory accumulates here
it is empty

an unremarkable box
a box abandoned in a taxi
cardboard makes it plain
it is otherwise obvious

a long box
a long box & a promise
a box no one doubts
an embrace is the same

a shallow box suggests a corset
a box into which teeth
& tears rattle soundlessly
no dream doubts this

a glass box
a shape that insinuates a mirror
a last box a box containing a ribbon
or about which a rhythm is tied

a gold box
a blue & green box
a box of iron or copper a gold box
a toothed box & fretted lid

Elise Ficarra

Counter-Spell to Inflect Fear

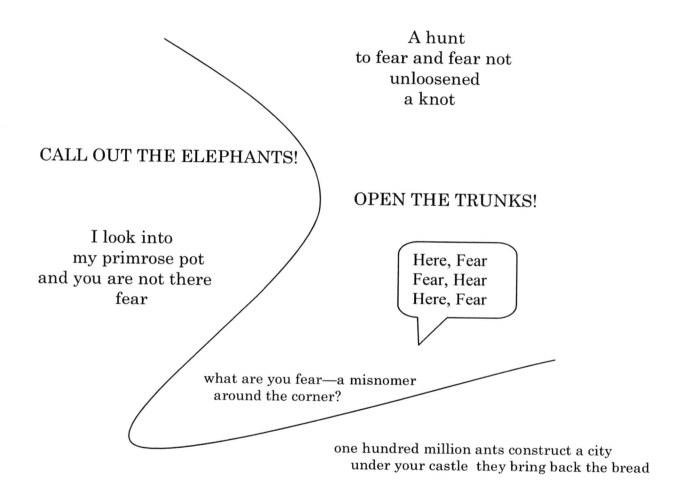

A hunt
to fear and fear not
unloosened
a knot

CALL OUT THE ELEPHANTS!

OPEN THE TRUNKS!

I look into
my primrose pot
and you are not there
fear

Here, Fear
Fear, Hear
Here, Fear

what are you fear—a misnomer
around the corner?

one hundred million ants construct a city
under your castle they bring back the bread

We Stomp Our Feet

Where Grown-ups Sleep

Point

A lamp illumines stairs and windows pillars roads

Oddball Aliens

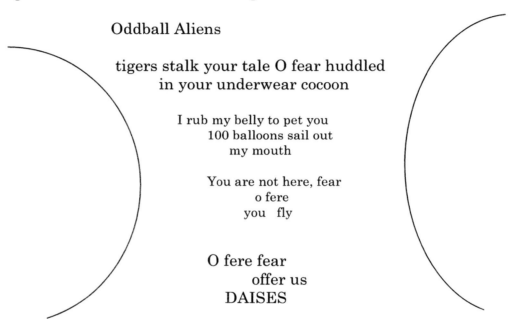

tigers stalk your tale O fear huddled
in your underwear cocoon

I rub my belly to pet you
100 balloons sail out
my mouth

You are not here, fear
o fere
you   fly

O fere fear
offer us
DAISES

His face lurks in a tree—A Green Green Kind Man with a mane
of leaves! He lives! He is not fear O face O fere. If his smile is sap
we sip it! He beams in the beams of the ceiling.

O Thief Fair Fear
You better Come Here—Don't get caught
Stealing the Washing!

OPTIMIZING FORMULA:

Pumpkin Sop
Bottle neck Blank side
Fat flicker — Lazy bee
Hackles of Jackals
Astronaut Orangutan
fiber optic microscopic
Slithering Snake

AWAKE!

COUNTERPOINT

Medusa, one of three, her snaky hair guards the lair where livid fear

That pinhead Perseus slew her but she was not a small cog wheel

the teeth of which fit into a larger gear She

was One of Three

**HAR
MON
IZE
THE
AN
IM
AL
S**

crawlingaroundthefurniture

Picture You
Here
Fear

*yourbreathtickles
myfancy*

**WIND
AND
UN
WIND
AND
RE
WIND
THE
REEL**

MELODY FREED
(skipping)

Jennifer Firestone

Valentine

I am your bestest friend
For ever and ever.
We will sky high
To 'wildering tops
Shattering snow
And blood leaves.
We will take
Wood bows
With arrows
And shock fat air.
Dare us
And we will concede.
We with blue
And feather height
Will sugar storm
Bird light
White a quiet tower.
We are one and two
Anew and flickering.
We sing
Apricot hues and
Huckleberry wisps.
We whisper
And glow nightly.
We rain shine
Our bows
And sing mightily:
Hi Ho Ho
The Wind Does Blow
But We
Are Never Frightened!

Akilah Oliver

Boulder, Colorado Poem 2

Canyon Street was once Water St.
I believe that's true though
a movement across diagonal borders could signal time
to say hello to slant sunrise.

I wouldn't recognize that tree in another
location, Los Angeles for example or the broad reach of
a train's whistle as if the
length of it were a vacation home I have yet to conquer.

Sam at the coffee shop talks of tagging,
still I am vacating that memory position as if it might
sneeze uncontrollably and make me an inappropriate
laugh machine tuned and forgotten,

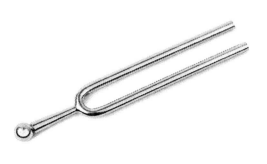

Tan Lin

Maybe

Sent & scented

U R a "swan" inside my
afternoon. It was

2:50 = river = plaid state
2:51 I'm in

a gymnasium = mint tea and chorizo hash > salvia
2:52 algebra plaid

plate (gas station)
(attendant)

Delirium gargoyles trinket a sweater in
a sweater I called cruciform

vegetables. I wrote "you"
in the bath tub. "NOTES"

about yr fleece & /yr math. Eleven dogs cried
the color of reptiles,

plus or minus the inside, then
hurt, Leffe in Antwerp, then the outside,

then temperature and a house
repeat a pattern in a tablecloth

and I am unvaried or a falling where
you and I are standing

Sent from iPhone
2:54 where

one r is /
I miss / you and I love you hum

one day's glow for nor
was a day before

I wrote a Lincoln and baked
myself awake

I swam all summer,
indeterminately

your oblong
comets

You: thumb velvet
in an indentation

of purring
2:53 & all my faces

2:54 (some articles of loathing)
(the Teflon in a river *

of milk

U R, November, what) is a year and a few
ellipses

) *) in a summer powder

R. Zamora Linmark

The Archaeology of Youth

When I was young, Grandpa warned me
about growing up. He taught me
all the ropes so I could skip
through life without stepping on any cords.

"Hijo," he said, "you're a smart jumper.
Just remember that for each birthday,
don't make a wish because wishes come too late.
Swallow the candles instead. That way,
nobody can take away the years."

So I did, wax melting inside me, making
me jump higher and higher until my body
broke through the corrugated tin roof.

One morning, Grandpa coughed up blood
the length of vines. When the doctor
said it was tuberculosis, he laughed and
said he was tending a garden in his lungs.

"For my grandson," he said, braiding the vines
into a cord as he spat them out.
Then he climbed into bed and jumped.
He jumped so high he never came back.

Now, whenever someone tells me to grow up,
I go to my room and pull the rope out
from between the mattresses. I jump,
and keep jumping until I see my grandfather
wearing a suit of vines and melting wax.

Yedda Morrison

Excerpted from **Minor Beasts In Translation**

(Note to big kids: All text is taken from the "On-Line Parallel Bible," a site that tracks numerous versions of the bible, line by line. Each sentence below beginning with a bold, capitalized letter represents a different translation or version of the same line.)

Sparrow

I watch, and have become like a sparrow that is alone on the housetop. **I** watch, and am become like a sparrow that is alone upon the housetop. **I** keep watch like a bird by itself on the housetop. **I** watch, and am like a sparrow alone upon the housetop. **I** watch, and am as a sparrow alone upon the housetop. **I** watch, and am become like a sparrow that is alone upon the housetop. **I** have watched, and I am as a bird alone on the roof.

Wild Donkey

The wild donkeys stand on the bare heights, they pant for air like jackals; their eyes fail, because there is no herbage. **A**nd the wild asses stand on the bare heights, they pant for air like jackals; their eyes fail, because there is no herbage. **A**nd the asses of the field on the open hilltops are opening their mouths wide like jackals to get air; their eyes are hollow because there is no grass. **A**nd the wild asses stand on the heights, they snuff up the wind like jackals; their eyes fail, because there is no herbage. **A**nd the wild asses did stand in the high places, they snuffed up the wind like dragons; their eyes did fail, because there was no grass. **A**nd the wild asses stand on the high hills, they gasp for air like jackals; their eyes fail, because there is no herbage. **A**nd wild asses have stood on high places, they have swallowed up wind like dragons, consumed have been their eyes, for there is no herb.

Dog

Thorns will come up in its palaces, nettles and thistles in its fortresses; and it will be a habitation of jackals, a court for ostriches. **A**nd thorns shall come up in its palaces, nettles and thistles in the fortresses thereof; and it shall be a habitation of jackals, a court for ostriches. **A**nd thorns will come up in her fair houses, and waste plants in her strong towers: and foxes will make their holes there, and it will be a meeting-place for ostriches. **A**nd thorns shall come up in her palaces, nettles and brambles in her fortresses; and it shall be a dwelling-place of wild dogs, a court for ostriches. **A**nd thorns shall come up in her palaces, nettles and brambles in the fortresses thereof: and it shall be an habitation of dragons, and a court for owls. **A**nd thorns shall come up in her palaces, nettles and thistles in the fortresses thereof; and it shall be a habitation of wild-dogs, an enclosure for ostriches. **A**nd gone up her palaces have thorns, nettle and bramble 'are' in her fortresses, and it hath been a habitation of dragons, a court for daughters of an ostrich.

Nest

The nursing child will play near a cobra's hole, and the weaned child will put his hand on the viper's den. And the sucking child shall play on the hole of the asp, and the weaned child shall put his hand on the adder's den. And the child at the breast will be playing by the hole of the snake, and the older child will put his hand on the bright eye of the poison-snake. And the sucking child shall play on the hole of the adder, and the weaned child shall put forth its hand to the viper's den. And the sucking child shall play on the hole of the asp, and the weaned child shall put his hand on the cockatrice's den. And the sucking child shall play on the hole of the asp, and the weaned child shall put his hand on the basilisk's den. And played hath a suckling by the hole of an asp, and on the den of a cockatrice hath the weaned one put his hand.

Raven

But the pelican and the porcupine will possess it. The owl and the raven will dwell in it. He will stretch the line of confusion over it, and the plumb line of emptiness. But the pelican and the porcupine shall possess it; and the owl and the raven shall dwell therein: and he will stretch over it the line of confusion, and the plummet of emptiness. But the birds of the wasteland will have their place there; it will be a heritage for the bittern and the raven: and it will be measured out with line and weight as a wasteland. And the pelican and the bittern shall possess it, and the great owl and the raven shall dwell in it. And he shall stretch out upon it the line of waste, and the plummets of emptiness. But the cormorant and the bittern shall possess it; the owl also and the raven shall dwell in it: and he shall stretch out upon it the line of confusion, and the stones of emptiness. But the pelican and the bittern shall possess it, and the owl and the raven shall dwell therein; and He shall stretch over it the line of confusion, and the plummet of emptiness. And possess her do pelican and hedgehog, and owl and raven dwell in her, and he hath stretched out over her a line of vacancy, and stones of emptiness.

Wolf

The wild animals of the desert will meet with the wolves, and the wild goat will cry to his fellow. Yes, the night creature shall settle there, and shall find herself a place of rest.

And the wild beasts of the desert shall meet with the wolves, and the wild goat shall cry to his fellow; yea, the night-monster shall settle there, and shall find her a place of rest.

And the beasts of the waste places will come together with the jackals, and the evil spirits will be crying to one another, even the night-spirit will come and make her resting-place there. And there shall the beasts of the desert meet with the jackals, and the wild goat shall cry to his fellow; the Lilith also shall settle there, and find for herself a place of rest.

The wild beasts of the desert shall also meet with the wild beasts of the island, and the satyr shall cry to his fellow; the screech owl also shall rest there, and find for herself a place of rest. And the wild-cats shall meet with the jackals, and the satyr shall cry to his fellow; yea, the night-monster shall repose there, and shall find her a place of rest. And met have Ziim with Aiim, And the goat for its companion calleth, only there rested hath the night-owl, and hath found for herself a place of rest.

Gazelle

The hart, and the gazelle, and the roebuck, and the wild goat, and the ibex, and the antelope, and the chamois. The hart, and the gazelle, and the roebuck, and the wild goat, and the pygarg, and the antelope, and the chamois. The hart, the gazelle, and the roe, the mountain goat and the pygarg and the antelope and the mountain sheep. The hart, and the gazelle, and the stag, and the wild goat, and the dishon and the oryx, and the wild sheep.

The hart, and the roebuck, and the fallow deer, and the wild goat, and the pygarg, and the wild ox, and the chamois. The hart, and the gazelle, and the roebuck, and the wild goat, and the pygarg, and the antelope, and the mountain sheep. Hart, and roe, and fallow deer, and wild goat, and pygarg, and wild ox, and chamois.

Leslie Scalapino

Breath-Memory

Three chapters excerpted from **The Dihedrons Gazelle-Dihedrals Zoom**

The plane

Gelechiid mistaken seen by the base runner in the gelid air of ice floods for gelechild he seeks to save on a far float gemsbok Oryx gazelle gemma budlike before his eyes run/ runs. Many taurine yet transmuting in sound tautosyllabic needless occurring in the same syllable the (s) and (t) are tautosyllabic in the word "disturb" needless but not needless in "distaste"—why not? as action constantly seeing things one silly doesn't understand or know—why not? It seems to be *that one's* core nature. But not his, is irrelevant to him. The base runner crosses the rime the forst forced forest freezing on the surface ahead only a jigger nothing before him for the figment of the gelechild now appears behind him when he happens chances to glance behind on the diamond twinkling. The base is ahead.

"Gemsbok"

"Gemsbok" he calls laughing at himself slipping on the frozen depth ice moving to on sea where the base runner departing from the huge outline has run to the gelechild freezing on the edge ice floats on which suddenly gemsbok stand or run beside the stationary gelechild who is actually moving rapidly away zoom(s?) in reverse forward before him as if leading him—the base runner stops, seeing the danger of the fast forest freezing ice flows at an emerald darkness where the side-dihedrons seem to flit though their actual movement at sides is omitted they simply appear elsewhere on the emerald edge (horizon). Since they cannot zoom to what would be forward for them? Or their zooming crossing for him horizontally is invisible to him. They oar they or the air does. A doe. Does then of gemsbok. The image sight of the gelechild breaks up in the seeing—in the eyes—of the base runner who is now exhausted spent panting lungs close (they close gills) to bursting streak of hot pain where he will begin to freeze at his core.

Breath-Memory

Breath-memory of a Siberian tracker is heard in his ear cautioning is breath-memory the same as flat-lining or rather opposite red fully dilated eye? "Hurry. Gather the stalks of the dead dry tall plants that lightly attach or unattach to the surface of the blowing giant frozen waste lake stacking them wild blowing horizontal grass tied as tying with only a minute or two to do so working fast he's bending cutting them in dusk with a scythe carried on his belt securing the stalks before the emerald horizon closes utterly freezing the heart's lake of the base runner inside grasped dreaming being held also in the warm engulfing grip of the Silvertip who'd seen him from the edge of its eye lake inside it."

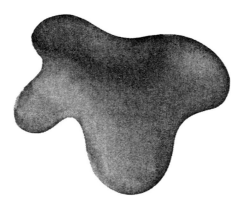

Donna de la Perrière

Surface Tension

I am trying to change my view of history,

positing something.

Words are maps or papers.

Pieces keep piling up.

I am still building into them their own destruction.

The seeds of that destruction.

I am having a hard time with this.

We just drove out to Salt Lake City.

The edge of the water begins about a hundred

yards beyond the edge of the spiral.

It was like snow.

It got deep very fast.

Everything got thick with salt.

(The world white in its harness.)

The water itself.

The weight of the water.

M. NourbeSe Philip

Excerpted from **Zong!**

Zong! #17

there was

        the this

        the that

        the frenzy

                leaky seas &

                  casks

                  negroes of no belonging

on board

no rest

        came the rains

        came the negroes

        came the perils

        came the owners

                master and mariners

Adunni, Akanni, Akanbi, Alade, Alayande

                                                            the this

                                                            the that

                                                            the frenzy

            came the insurance of water

            water of good only

            came water sufficient

            that was truth

            & seas of mortality

                                        question the now

                                    the this

                                    the that

                                    the frenzy

            not unwisely

_____

Ayoka, Faluyi, Owolabi, Oni, Sowole, Dehinde

Will Alexander

Excerpted from **Across The Vapour Gulf**

*

It is night, and the plasma of the Sun is seeping through its lunar mists
of imaginary lions.

*

Ghost travel, intimate water travel, the telepathic intuitives of a finely muted
turquoise perspective.

*

Now, just as quickly, tempestuous refractions of the heart, partaking of an unceasing
alien hypnotic, reflecting a mental state, part quantum, part supra, trembling at the cusp
of an a-carnal lake, breaking, through anticipatory assumptives, having done with issues
which evolve from distractive embarrassment.

*

Yes, the blue majestical birds of eternity, their wings, like the burning manes
of magical citron ponies, wheeling around a sudden helium vapour, as if,
at the centre of a great cerulean hive, witness to intangible Sanskrit Suns,
as powerful witness to trenchant combinatory balance.

**Lee Ann Brown
& Miranda Torn**

On Organic Form

It's the tree's choice

what the treehouse looks like

in the end

Sarah Rosenthal

Conjecture

If we're all
trying on the same
swim suits and

accepting even
complimenting
each other

maybe the soul
of a person
is shaped like

a tear drop
or rose bud
a fullness ready

for the heat
stage, maybe a
group is like

that waiting to
swim and then
eat, my suit's

rose pink shockingly
attractive as everyone
thinks

Susana Gardner

Shores

Shores Shores I shores in Shores Shores I shores
in Shores Inn Shores Is Shores Shores I shores in
Shores Inn Shores Is Shores Shores I shores in
Shores Inn Shores Is Shores Shores I shores in
Shores Inn Shores Is Shores Inn Shores Is Shores
Shores I shores in Shores Inn Shores Is Shore in
Horses I Horses I Horses In Sun Horses Inn Us
Horses Sin Horses Ins Hearses Her Seas Horses Is
Hers is Herso is Shore

Bruce Covey

Circles

⌐ı uıc ⸴
ues, the pres
l short video r
ry, could repe'
'ds is bet⁺

...⸴, ...ı⸴
⸴ was that the sou.
⸴ hand built this huge w
:k, so too does atmosphei
ary maintains the Circle N
⸴iduals, groups, networks,
⸴e world. Every thing lo
'⸴, spreading its little
·ıght. This in'

. ⸴⸴
showing hı
ns spiritual p
⸴de or implie
⁺ance—

.⸴ ⸴ı
with their typic⸴
⸴ a segment, radically ⸴
ıı are considerable and th
w each other. The man fiı
ills the sky. Politely carrı
·atter. We appreciate the
'ıpment of least restrı
·ıding the dileı·

⸴sposed upoıı
ıısed shadow. We belı⸴
ıgh age eight are at a formatı
ıd! how final! how it puts a ne⸴·
ı past the fountain, electing not to
ıral-philosophical, and research b⸴
models for young children with dı·
ıarel became blanketed with silı,
by that which follows. Electı·
·ır gathered backwards. Lı'
·ıd every dew drop
¹·· ·ın tⁿ·

ıourney
ıoon gets wo
ıd presently, ⸴
·ious ladder ·
·ınsiⁿ·

Juan Felipe Herrera

Nakkaloo
the girl who lived in a Hip-Hop shoe

One frosty night while eating
Chilaquiles con salsa
And Pupusas filled with frijoles
And a super tall glass of atole
I heard The Squeaky things
Those nasty negative noodle headed nah-nah-nahs
Those squeaky things that pour out of everywhere
When you least expect them — sometimes here, sometimes
There and there and there!

Hanna!
Hanna!
Hanna!

Tell them your name isn't Hanna
Tell them your name isn't famous!
Tell them your name is kinda lame-ous!
So tell them all your name if you dare!
So tell them where you live
and just watch 'em stare!

You're no Hanna!
You're no Hanna!
You're Hanna!
And you're no fun-ah!

I can hear the squeakies from my shoe.
My been-living-here-for-a-little-while-shoe.
My we just came from the other side
ridin' all the way to this side on a dollar shoe!

But that's ok cause today I met a girl
And her name is Sharmel that's all I am gonna tell
Sharmel tall Sharmel skinny like Sharmel very very funny

Well, what's your name?
Sharmel said... tell me once tell me twice
I bet you it's really nice like toasty roasty red beans and rice

My name is… Nakkaloo from Ixtapa!
What kinda talka is that kinda talka?
I said my name is Nakkaloo from Ixtapa!
NakaNakaNaka!
Plicka-Plaka-Plicka-Plooka-Plaka!
Plicka-Plaka-Plicka-Plooka-Plaka!

The Squeaky Things
Ha-ha-ha!
Hee-hee-hee!
Ha-ha-ha!

Hey, hey! That sounds like uh, Hip-Hop!

She don't know how to Hip-Hop!
She don't know how to make it rock!
She don't know cuz she lives in a freaky funky sock!

Hippy-hop-hop-hop-ah?
I don't live in a sock I don't live on a rock
I live in a shoe where I make my stew habichuela
Good for your muela almost Cinderella like my abuela Mela said

The Squeaky Things -

Plicka-Plaka-Plicka-Plooka-Plaka!
Plicka-Plaka-Plicka-Plooka-Plaka!

Ha!
Ha!

What's all that plicka plaka rappa'
Sharmel said so instead I danced a really cool tappa'
And I said as I tapp-ad

Plicka placka is the hoppin' sound hoppin' all the steps
I hopped and I stepped
Stepping all the way from Ixtapa
That's the sound of this fancy shoe I found

What?

What?

Floating underneath the Golden Gate Bridge
Where I made a wish – I wish I wish I wish…

Wish?

Sharmel turned around and spun on the ground –

Oh, what did you wish, Nakkaloo?
Did you wish for a dish of split pea stew?
Did you wish for a dish of buggar-sized Cheetos and
Bugger-size Fritos? That's too extreme makes me wanna scream!
Oh, Nakkaloo, Nakkaloo, Oh, tell me it isn't true!

So I said walking to my shoe:

The shoe was lonely like me you see,
Far from its land on the other side like me,
No one wanted it. No one thought of it. No one polished it.

But I wanted it. I thought of it. I polished it.

Is that the-the-the shoe where you live?
I thought you were kidding, girl! What in the world?

The Squeaky Things -
No!
Oh, yeah?

So?
Oh, yeah?

The Squeaky Things -
Nakkaloo lives in a shoe that's so uncool would you?
Nakkaloo lives in a shoe that's so uncool would you?

Sharmel couldn't tell the Squeaky things from the trees:

Did you hear something, Nakkaloo?
Kinda of a buncha cruncha squeaky things?

I hear them all the time. When you live in a shoe like I do…
Everybody kinda laughs at you and makes weird noises, it's so true!

I won't laugh at you, Nakkaloo. No way Nakkaloo!
Well, Nakkaloo? What kinda wish did you wish,
After you polished your shoe by the Golden Gate Bridge?

So I Hippied and I Hoppa'd and I sang
to Sharmel with a hoppin' twang…

I want a friend, like in Ixtapa!
        Skipping up the hills to the sky
I want a friend, like in Ixtapa!
        Ticklin' me when I play on the waters splashing high
I want a friend, like in Ixtapa!
        Counting all the sparkles of the city made of moonlight

The Squeaky Voices -
Plicka Placka!
Plicka Plooka Plaka! Plicka Phooey!
Plicka Placka!
Plicka Plooka Plaka! Plicka Phooey!

So Sharmel took my hand and we skipped for a while
And the winds tossed our hair and for a while we weren't anywhere
We flew to the hills past the bay and then Sharmel and me turned around
In a skinny second and a dancing way and then she smiled

The Squeaky Things -
Plicka Placka!
Plicka Plooka Plaka! Plicka Phooey!
Plicka Placka!

San Francisco is kinda like Ixtapa, I said
I was lookin' at it all, all the time
And all the way but when you held my hand
I, I, I wasn't afraid, Sharmel, I wasn't afraid
I guess, you're kinda my best friend, Sharmel, I guess…

Sharmel said… You guess?
Just kinda?

Then I turned red-red and orange like a plate of enchiladas
And I blew out a steamy breath like a pupusa when it gets too hot-ah
And I said:

Not kinda, Sharmel, can't you tell?
You are my best new amiga friend a whole buncha buncha!
No one has ever invited me to play, like you did today

The Squeaky Things
Plicka Plooka Plaka! Phooeeey

Then I sang like in a Hip-Hop dance:

> I was looking for a place to land
> Traveling far from home in a polished Hip-Hop shoe
> Crissin' and a crossin'
> Floating and a tossin'
> I am telling you so true
> Wonderin' if I'd ever find a friend again!

The Squeaky Voices -
Plicka Placka!
Plicka Plooka Plaka! Plicka Phooey!
Plicka Placka!
Plicka Plooka Plaka! Plicka Phooey!

Then Sharmel took out some flores from her back-pack
and a Collard Green snack an all
She knocked on the door on the side of my shoe
and stood very tall
Buenas tardes, Señora, she said I
just came here to say
I wish Nakkaloo and all of you will stay
Here's some greens for you
Cuz I am new from Arkansas
And when I saw Nakkaloo I guess I knew
I was not the only lonely one too
Please say you'll stay and not ever go away!

Then my Mama and My papa came out and sang!
Ok! Ok! Ok!
And I took Sharmel by the hand and we danced!

Hippin' and a Hoppin' from Ixtapa
In a Hip-Hop shoe made just for me and you
Friends crissin' and a crossin'
Hearing squeaky things not wanting us to sing
All the way to the Golden Gate painted like an enchilada
Hippin' and a-Hoppin' all the way from Ixtapa
Never   gonna
Stoppa!

The Squeaky Things
Never
gonna
stoppa!

And we never did stop Hippin' and a-Hoppin and our Hip-Hop Shoe shined under the Golden Gate Bridge for all to see...

Sweet Angelmouth

OKAY

Underneath the lilac tree
I found a place to comfort me

That's where I went
To shed my fears
And cry until I had no tears

A kitten followed
To my lap
Beneath the lilacs we would nap

The bees would buzz around my nose
The moss was cooling to my toes
The flowers smelled so sweet of spring

IMAGINE IT

I felt that maybe everything
Was going to be okay again

I knew things couldn't always go
The way I wanted
Even so

If only things could be okay
That's all I wanted
Anyway

Rachel Levitsky

Excerpted from **Basement, Basement Window**

Dear Nicolas,

In a conversation with the wind and rain throughout the night I asked the wind and the rain if it were a mouse and why did it find me so alone? The rain told me I was lazy and the wind told me *to be afraid*. I went to the window when I woke and I asked the rain and the wind about my day. They told me, "It is ruined. You are sad. You may as well write that story about a boy in the world." I told the rain and the wind, "From my window the world looks so small but still, I cannot understand it, even in the miniature that is my personal view of the street below." I made strong coffee. "What am I forgetting?" I asked the rain, now having taken over the scene for the most part. "You are forgetting to breathe and to listen very carefully. Ignore the mean wind when it bellows loudly and teaches you fear. Sit down, write, read, eat your green grapes."

Love,
Rachel

Kevin Killian

Water Colors

In Brooklyn we flipped Necco Wafers with our thumbnails
from the table's edge to a glass of water standing between us in the diner booth

> Watch closely as wafer after wafer gives up its bruised secret of water colors, pale pink, dusty orange, cocoa brown, and that green, the green of pistachio ice cream… We have come so far that

In order to get to you, Jeanne, what a strange path I had to take!

—so long to come to you

> In the passageway I squeezed past his enormous brim and into the porthole where, lay waiting, like a snake crawling from the left edge of the page to the right, then bounding back

"Pour arriver jusqu'à toi, quel drôle de chemin j'ai dû prendre."

That was where I was going when the call came

to shut down the shop

> In Flatbush my grandfather ruled the halls of Bushwick High, a ruler in his hand, not your regular 12 inch ruler but an 18 incher, students quaked when they saw him come your way, the fear whitening their eyebrows and sideburns like Macaulay Culkin

This was the principal's grandson of the royal house of Killian

when taken, the medicine goes up the down staircase,

> The side effects closed on my nose

Clock ticks on

It took me such a long time to catch this busy coach to Yuma

where, we were on a Greyhound bus and Robin Thomas, the perfect name for him, slept on my lap all night long his head piled high with dreams and water colors

Robin Blaser

8:25pm - Nov. 6, 2006

I like to talk to moonlight

when the fog lets it out

I like to say, "How are you?"

answering to the calm light

of it   -   wow! stick to the dark

of this and whisper, "next

time, dear light of this"

December 16, 2006

don't let the world be

without you

grab a hold on it

and swing

as far out in the heart

and mind of it

as you can reach

that's where your words

seek the marvelous

and speak day and night

Author Biographies

Poet and performer **Akilah Oliver** (1961–2011) was born in L.A. where in the 1990's, she founded and performed with the feminist performance collective Sacred Naked Nature Girls. Her published work includes the volumes *A Toast In The House of Friends* (Coffee House, 2009) and *the she said dialogues: flesh memory* (Smokeproof/Erudite Fangs, 1999) and the chapbooks *An Arriving Guard of Angels, Thusly Coming to Greet* (Farfalla, McMillan & Parrish, 2004), *The Putterer's Notebook* (Belladonna, 2006), *"a(A)ugust"* (Yo-Yo Labs, 2007) and *A Collection of Objects* (Tente, 2010). She was artist-in-residence at Beyond Baroque Literary Arts Center in Los Angeles and recipient of grants from California Arts Council, The Flintridge Foundation, and the Rockefeller Foundation. She was an instructor at Naropa University, The New School, and Pratt Institute and traveled widely to perform her texts with musicians and collaborators and to give workshops. Akilah Oliver was also an active member of the Belladonna* Collaborative and a PhD candidate at The European Graduate School, for which she was completing a book-length theory of lamentation.

Andrew Choate is a South Carolinian by nature but has been writing in Los Angeles since 2001. He studied music and language at Northwestern and CalArts. His first book, *Langquage Makes Plastic of the Body*, was published by Palm Press in 2006, and his most recent book, *Stingray Clapping*, was published by Insert Blanc Press in 2012. His radio plays have been broadcast on WDR in Germany and RAI in Italy; his artwork has been exhibited in Yerevan, London, and Los Angeles. He was interviewed in the February 2011 issue of *Facsimile Magazine*.

Anne Waldman—poet, performer, professor, editor, and cultural activist—is the author of more than forty books of poetry. She is also the co-editor of numerous anthologies including *Civil Disobediences: Poetics and Politics in Action* and *Beats at Naropa*. She is the co-founder with Allen Ginsberg of the renowned Jack Kerouac School of Disembodied Poetics at the Naropa University in Boulder, Colorado, where she is Chair and Artistic Director of The Summer Writing Program. She has been one of the prime movers and creators of the "Outrider" experimental poetry community for over four decades. Waldman has worked actively for social change and has devoted her life to poetry and artistic "community."

Beverly Dahlen's work includes four volumes of the open-ended series *A Reading*, the most recently published of which is *A Reading 18-20* (Instance Press, 2006). *A Reading: Birds* has been published as a chapbook by Little Red Leaves Editions new "Textile Series," edited and designed by Dawn Pendergast. Ms. Dahlen has also published widely in numerous periodicals and anthologies.

Bhanu Kapil has written four books: *The Vertical Interrogation of Strangers* (Kelsey Street Press), *Incubation: a space for monsters* (Leon Works), *humanimal[a project for future children]* (Kelsey Street Press), and *Schizophrene* (Nightboat Books.) She teaches at Naropa and Goddard.

Brent Cunningham is a writer, publisher, and visual artist currently living in Oakland with his wife and daughter. His first book, *Bird & Forest*, was published by Ugly Duckling Presse in 2005; his second book, *Journey to the Sun*, was published by Atelos in 2012. He and Neil Alger are the founders of Hooke Press, a chapbook press dedicated to publishing short runs of poetry, criticism, theory, writing, and ephemera.

Brian Strang lives in Oakland. He is the author of *INCRETION* (Spuyten Duyvil), *MACHINATIONS* (a free Duration ebook), and several chapbooks. Recent poem/paintings can be seen at his website, *Sorry Nature*, and at *Deep Oakland*. He has had three solo shows of his paintings, and his poems, translations, reviews, and essays have appeared in many journals including *New American Writing, The Denver Quarterly, Caliban*, and (translated) in the Portuguese journal *Diversos*.

Bruce Covey is the author of five books of poetry, including *Reveal: All Shapes & Sizes* (Bitter Cherry, 2012), *Glass Is Really a Liquid* (No Tell Books, 2010), and *Elapsing Speedway Organism* (No Tell, 2006). He lives in Atlanta, Georgia, where he edits *Coconut Poetry* and curates the *What's New in Poetry* reading series.

CA Conrad's childhood included selling cut flowers along the highway for his mother and helping her shoplift. He is the author of *A BEAUTIFUL MARSUPIAL AFTERNOON: New (Soma)tics* (Wave Books, 2012), *The Book of Frank* (Wave Books, 2010), *Advanced Elvis Course* (Soft Skull Press, 2009), *Deviant Propulsion* (Soft Skull Press, 2006), and a collaboration with poet Frank Sherlock titled *The City Real & Imagined* (Factory School, 2010). He is a 2011 Pew Fellow, a 2012 Ucross Fellow, and a 2013 BANFF Fellow. He is the editor of the online video poetry journals *JUPITER 88* and *Paranormal Poetics*. Visit him at CAConrad.blogspot.com.

Camille Roy is a writer and performer. Her most recent book is *Sherwood Forest*, from Futurepoem. Earlier books include *Cheap Speech*, a play, from Leroy, and *Craquer*, a fictional autobiography from 2nd Story Books, as well as *Swarm* (two novellas, Black Star Series), among others. She co-edited *Biting The Error: Writers Explore Narrative* (Coach House, 2005, re-issued 2010). Roy has taught creative writing at San Francisco State University, California State University SummerArts, and Naropa.

Cathy Park Hong's first book, *Translating Mo'um*, was published in 2002 by Hanging Loose Press. Her second collection, *Dance Dance Revolution*, was chosen for the Barnard Women Poets Prize and was published in 2007 by WW Norton. Her third book of poems, *Engine Empire*, was published in May 2012 by WW Norton. Hong is also the recipient of a Fulbright Fellowship and a National Endowment for the Arts Fellowship. Her poems have been published in *A Public Space, Poetry, Paris Review, Conjunctions, McSweeney's, Harvard Review, Boston Review, The Nation, American Letters & Commentary, Denver Quarterly*, and other journals. She is a Professor at Sarah Lawrence College.

Charles Bernstein is author of *All the Whiskey in Heaven: Selected Poems* (Farrar, Straus and Giroux, 2010) and *The Attack of the Difficult Poems: Essays & Inventions* (University of Chicago, 2011). He is Regan Professor of English and Comparative Literature at the University of Pennsylvania. "Emma's Nursery Rimes" were written for and with Emma Bee Bernstein (1985–2008).

Christian Bök is the author not only of *Crystallography* (Coach House Press, 1994), a pataphysical encyclopedia nominated for the Gerald Lampert Memorial Award, but also of *Eunoia* (Coach House Books, 2001), a best-selling work of experimental literature, which has gone on to win the Griffin Prize for Poetic Excellence. *Utne Reader* has recently included Bök in its list of "50 Visionaries Who Are Changing Your World." Bök teaches English at the University of Calgary.

Claire Blotter writes and performs poetry with movement & body rhythms and represented San Francisco in National Poetry Slams in Boston and Chicago in the early '90s. She has been published in such diverse journals as *Barnwood, Gargoyle, Canary,* and the *We'Moon Datebooks*. Her most recent poetry chapbook, *The Moment House,* is forthcoming from Finishing Line Press. She teaches in the Independent Study Program at Tamalpias High School and in the California Poets in the Schools and Poetry Out Loud Programs. Her award-winning video documentary, *Wake-up Call: Saving the Songbirds,* about the worldwide decline of migratory songbirds is distributed by the Video Project.

Dana Teen Lomax is the author of *Disclosure* (Black Radish Books), *Ubu Edition #43* (UbuWeb), *Rx* (Dusie), *Curren¢y* (Palm Press), *Room* (a+bend), and co-editor of *Letters to Poets* (Saturnalia Books). Her work has appeared in *Jacket, Poets & Writers, The Bay Poetics Anthology* and *Against Expression*. She served as the Director of Small Press Traffic and is proud to be the editor of *Kindergarde*. She was excited to collaborate with her identical twin sister on their poem for this anthology.

Danna Lomax believes strongly in the transformative power of public education. A middle school bilingual teacher for nearly 20 years, she creates project-based units that encourage students to think critically about ways to make peace with themselves, each other, and the environment. Danna's awards include a Fulbright Teacher Scholarship, an AAUW Career Development Grant, and a PBS Innovation Award. She is currently exploring peace education with middle schoolers and pursuing an MA in Teaching and Curriculum from Fresno Pacific University. She lives in Southern California with her loving, supportive partner, their two unique and wondrous middle schoolers, five aloof kitties, and a Lucky dog.

Donna de la Perrière is the author of *Saint Erasure* (Talisman House, 2010) and *True Crime* (Talisman House, 2009). Her work has appeared in *No Gender: Reflections on the Life and Work of kari edwards* (Litmus Press, 2009), *Bay Poetics* (Faux Press, 2006), and numerous journals. The recipient of a 2009 Fund for Poetry Award, she teaches in the MFA and undergraduate creative writing programs at California College of the Arts and San Francisco State University, curates the Bay Area Poetry Marathon reading series at The Lab gallery and performance space in San Francisco's Mission District, and lives near downtown Oakland. Read more at www.donnadelaperriere.net.

Douglas Kearney is a poet, performer, librettist, and educator. His first full-length collection of poems, *Fear, Some*, was published in 2006 (Red Hen Press). His second manuscript, *The Black Automaton*, was selected by Catherine Wagner for the National Poetry Series (Fence Books, 2009) and was a finalist for the PEN America Award in Poetry (2010). www.douglaskearney.com

Duriel E. Harris is the author of *Drag* (Elixir Press), *Amnesiac: Poems* (Sheep Meadow Press), and *Speleology*, a collaboration with video artist Scott Rankin. A poet/performer, sound artist and scholar, Harris is a member of Douglas Ewart and Inventions free jazz ensemble, and co-founder of Black Took Collective. Current projects include the *AMNESIAC* media art project and *"Thingification,"* a solo play in one act. She is an associate professor of English and teaches creative writing and poetics at Illinois State University.

Edwin Torres is a bi-lingualisualist rooted in the languages of both sight and sound. His books include *Yes Thing No Thing* (Roof Books) and *One Night: Poems For The Sleepy* (Red Glass Books), among others. He has work in the forthcoming anthologies *The Heath Anthology of American Literature, Vol. E 7th Edition* (Cenguage Learning) and *Postmodern American Poetry Vol. 2* (Norton). The first fourteen words of his poem in *Kindergarde* came from his four-year-old son.

Eileen Myles's *Snowflake/different streets* (poems) came out in 2012 from Wave Books. She's published seventeen other books in the past three decades including *Inferno (a poet's novel)* in 2010 from orbooks.com. She received a Guggenheim Fellowship in 2012. She lives in New York.

Elise Ficarra is a Bay Area poet and writer. Her book *Swelter* won the Michael Rubin Book Award in 2005. She is a contributor to *hinge,* a BOAS anthology of experimental women writers. Her work can be found in various publications including *Birddog, Dusie, Eleven Eleven, Esque, Octopus, 26,* and *14 Hills.* She was an affiliate artist at Headlands Center for the Arts from June 2006–2008. She is associate director of The Poetry Center at SFSU.

Elizabeth Treadwell's *Kindergarde* piece is part of her most recent book, *Virginia or the mud-flap girl* (2012). Her earlier books include *Birds & Fancies* (2007) and *Chantry* (2004). She and her daughters, Ivy & Gemma, are often working on books of drawings and poems. For more info, visit elizabethtreadwell.com.

Erin Wilson's writing has appeared in various places, including the journals *Artiface, With+Stand, Typo,* and *Bird Dog,* and the books *hinge* (Crack Press, 2002) and *Building is a Process/Light is an Element* (P-Queue/Queue Books, 2008). She is a librarian and lives in Berkeley, California.

Etel Adnan, a native of Lebanon, is a poet, painter, and essayist. She lives in Paris, Beirut, and the San Francisco Bay Area where she taught philosophy at Dominican College. She is the author of many books of prose and poetry available in English, French, and Arabic. Her novel about the Civil War in Lebanon, *Sitt Marie-Rose* (Post-Apollo Press, 1982), won the Amitié Franco-Arab Prize (an award given by the Association de Solidarité Franco-Arabe) in 1977 and is considered a classic of Middle Eastern Literature. Recent works include *Seasons* (Post-Apollo Press, 2008), *Master of the Eclipse* (Interlink World Fiction, 2009), and *In the Heart of the Heart of Another Country* (City Lights, 2005).

Evie Shockley is the author of four collections of poetry—*the new black* (Wesleyan, 2011), *a half-red sea* (Carolina Wren Press, 2006), and two chapbooks—and a critical study *Renegade Poetics: Black Aesthetics and Formal Innovation in African American Literature* (Iowa, 2011). Among the honors and support Shockley's work has recently received is the 2012 Holmes National Poetry Prize. She teaches African American literature and creative writing at Rutgers University-New Brunswick.

Flora Beatrice Breitbard is Kit Robinson's granddaughter. She was five years old when "The Happy Onions" was written, but now she is seven. Flora lives with her parents in Oakland.

Garrett Caples is the author of two full-length poetry collections: *The Garrett Caples Reader* (1999) and *Complications* (2007). His book of essays, *Retrievals,* is forthcoming from Wave Books. He is the poetry editor at City Lights Books and a contributing writer to the *San Francisco Bay Guardian.* He is also the co-editor of the *Collected Poems of Philip Lamantia* (University of California, 2013).

Former debutant and Richmond, Virginia, native **giovanni singleton** edits *nocturnes (re)view,* a journal of literary and artistic experiments from the African Diaspora and other contested spaces. Her work has appeared in *Callaloo, VOLT, Zen Monster, Best of Fence,* and is forthcoming in *Writing Self and Community: A Norton Anthology of African American Poetry Since the Civil Rights Movement.* Her *AMERICAN LETTERS* series was selected for San Francisco's first Visual Poetry and Performance Festival. She watches deer, collects bookmarks, and enjoys figs.

Harryette Mullen teaches American poetry, African American literature, and creative writing at UCLA. Her poems, short stories, and essays have been published widely. Her poems have been translated into Spanish, Portuguese, French, Polish, Swedish, Turkish, Bulgarian, Danish, and Italian. She is the author of several poetry books, most recently *Recyclopedia* (Graywolf, 2006), winner of a PEN Beyond Margins Award, and *Sleeping with the Dictionary* (University of California, 2002), a finalist for a National Book Award, National Book Critics Circle Award, and Los Angeles Times Book Prize. Her most recent publication is an essay collection, *The Cracks Between* (University of Alabama, 2012). Her work-in-progress, a tanka diary, is due in 2013.

Writer and visual artist **Jaime Cortez** has exhibited at the Oakland Museum, the Berkeley Art Museum, Galería de la Raza, and Intersection for the Arts. His short stories and essays have been published in more than a dozen anthologies including *Street Art San Francisco, Besame Mucho,* and *Best Gay Erotica 2.* He edited the anthology *Virgins, Guerrillas & Locas* and created the graphic novel *Sexile/Sexilio. On the Job,* his graphic novel about his father's checkered work history, is his current project.

Jane Sprague's books include *The Port of Los Angeles* and *Imaginary Syllabi.* Her essays, poems, and chapbooks have been published in various print and online journals. Current projects include *My Appalachia,* a book about generational poverty, legacies of genocide, neglected rural people and places in upstate New York. She lives with her family on a manufactured island in Long Beach, California.

jared hayes tends to shadows and their ghosts in Portland, Oregon. hayes is the author of *The Dead Love* (Black Radish Books) and *Bandit* (Little Red Leaves Textile Series). he enjoys being in the company of the Dusie Kollektiv, Black Radish Books, and Livestock Editions. jared's poetry can be found.

Jeanne Lance has published four chapbooks of poetry and short prose. Her writing has appeared in *6ix, Autumn Harvest, Red Wheelbarrow,* and numerous other magazines. For many years, she co-edited *Gallery Works,* a literary and art publication, and coordinated readings at Intersection in San Francisco and Ear Inn in NYC. She is a member of a long-standing Poetry Salon—founded by the late Mark Linenthal—in the SF Bay Area. She recently proofread a volume of historical fiction by children, published by *StoneSoup,* based in Santa Cruz.

Jennifer Firestone is the author of *Flashes* (Shearsman Books), *Holiday* (Shearsman Books), and the chapbooks *Waves* (Portable Press at Yo-Yo Labs), *from Flashes* (Sona Books), and *snapshot* (Sona Books). She is the co-editor of *Letters To Poets: Conversations about Poetics, Politics and Community* (Saturnalia Books). She is an assistant professor of Literary Studies at the New School's Eugene Lang College. She lives with her husband and three children in Brooklyn.

Poet, publisher, and parent **Jill Stengel** founded a+bend press in 1999. She later added a journal, *mem*, featuring writing by poet-mothers raising young children. Several of Jill's serial poems have appeared in chapbook form; a selection can be viewed online at www.dusie.org. Her writing has also appeared in print and online journals and anthologies, including *Boog City, Shampoo, Traffic, Try*, and *Touched by Adoption*. Jill lives in Davis, California, with her computer-guy husband, three language-loving children, two cats, one dog, and a hermit crab.

Joan Larkin's poetry includes *Legs Tipped with Small Claws* (Argos Books), *My Body: New and Selected Poems* (Hanging Loose), *Cold River, A Long Sound,* and *Housework.* She edited *Gay and Lesbian Poetry in Our Time* with the late Carl Morse, and has taught at Brooklyn College, Drew University, and Sarah Lawrence, among many other places. Her honors include Lambda and Audre Lorde Awards, the Shelley Memorial Award, and the Academy of American Poets Fellowship.

Joan Retallack's *Procedural Elegies / Western Civ Cont'd /* was named a best book of 2010 by *ARTFORUM*. She is the author of eight books of poetry and a number of critical volumes including *The Poethical* Wager and *MUSICAGE: John Cage in Conversation with Joan Retallack,* which received the 1996 America Award in Belles-Lettres. Retallack has received a Lannan Poetry Award and NEA funding for an Artist's Book project. She has performed in and served as dramaturge for numerous Cage productions. Retallack is the John D. and Catherine T. MacArthur Professor of Humanities at Bard College.

Jocelyn Saidenberg is the author of *Mortal City* (Parentheses Writing Series), *CUSP* (Kelsey St. Press), *Negativity* (Atelos), and *Dispossessed* (Belladonna). She lives in San Francisco.

Johanna Drucker is the inaugural Martin and Bernard Breslauer Professor of Bibliographical Studies in UCLA's Department of Information Studies. She has written and lectured widely on topics related to the history of the book, with special emphasis on artists' books, typography, experimental poetry, and contemporary art. In addition to her scholarly work, Drucker is known as a book artist and writer whose works often make use of experimental typography and her work is in museum and library collections worldwide.

Jonas Brash and **Samantha Giles** live in Oakland, California, where they spend many afternoons talking about strange contraptions, Greek myths, and what kind of game shows their pets might create. Brash was in first grade when these poems were written and Giles was Director of Small Press Traffic.

Starting out as a farmworker child, grad of Bryant, Marshall and Patrick Henry SF Elementary Schools, and choir boy, **Juan Felipe** has written many books in poetry, novels in verse, children's books, and musicals such as the new *Stars of Juarez.* Recently, he garnered various awards including the Guggenheim Fellowship, the National Book Critics Circle Award, and the PEN Oakland-Josephine Miles National Literary Awards. He is professor of poetry at UC-Riverside and Poet Laureate of California.

Juliana Spahr lives in Berkeley.

Julie Ezelle Patton is the author of *Notes for Some (Nominally) Awake* and *A Garden Per Verse (or What Else do You Expect from Dirt?).* Her work has been anthologized in *((eco(lang)(uage(reader))* and *I'll Drown My Book: Conceptual Writing By Women* (Les Figues). Julie's performance art, featured at the Stone, Jazz Standard, and other noted international venues, emphasizes improvisation, collaboration, and other worldy chora-graphs. She is the founder of Poet Tree Mitigation, Ink, a native tree planting service, the Salon des Refuse, and Bluestone Circle artist housing project foregrounding utilitarian eco-arts, ritual maintenance work in America's rust belt. Julie has been honored with an Acadia Arts Foundation Grant and a New York Foundation for the Arts Fellowship (Poetry). Julie has taught at the Cooper Union for the Advancement of Science and Art, Naropa Univeristy's Jack Kerouac School of Disembodied Poetics, Schule fur Dichtung, and New York University. She lives in New York City.

Julien Poirier was born in Berkeley, California in 1970. After graduating from college in New York City, he traveled the world. He was lucky enough to be hired by Ucan Balon Kindergarten in Istanbul in 1997. He then returned to New York, spending 10 years as a public school poetry teacher with Learning through Expanded Arts Program (LEAP). He remains loyal to the U.S. public school, the future of America's mind-blowing art and poetry.

Kaia Sand is the author of *Remember to Wave* (Tinfish Press, 2010), a poetry book based on a walk Sand leads in Portland. She is the author of *interval* (Edge Books, 2004) and co-author with Jules Boykoff of *Landscapes of Dissent* (Palm Press, 2008). She wrote a magic show for both children and adults, *A Tale of Magicians Who Puffed Up Money that Lost its Puff.* She sews some poems, including an 8-foot embroidered dropcloth.

Kenneth Goldsmith is the author of ten books of poetry and is the founding editor of the online archive UbuWeb. He lives in New York City and teaches writing at the University of Pennsylvania.

Kevin Killian is a San Francisco writer. His books include *Bedrooms Have Windows, Shy, Little Men, Arctic Summer, Argento Series, I Cry Like a Baby,* and *Action Kylie.* His new novel is called *Spreadeagle* (from Publication Studio, Portland). As a child his favorite books were the *Oz* books, the *Alice* books, *Judy Bolton, Penrod and Sam, The Secret Garden, Freddy the Pig, Edward Eager,* and the *Beany Malone* books of Lenora Mattingly Weber.

Kit Robinson is the author of *Determination* (Cuneiform, 2010), *The Messianic Trees: Selected Poems, 1976–2003* (Adventures in Poetry, 2009), and 18 other books of poetry. He lives in Berkeley, where he works as a freelance writer and plays Cuban tres guitar in the Latin dance band Bahía Son.

Kristin Palm lives in Oakland where, as you may have guessed, she runs around Lake Merritt and watches urban birds.

Lee Ann Brown's books of poetry include *Polyverse, The Sleep That Changed Everything,* and *In the Laurels. Caught.* She lives in New York City where she teaches poetry at St. John's University and in Marshall, North Carolina, where she directs the French Broad Institute (of Time and the River), a space for poetry and performance. She is publisher of Tender Buttons, which publishes experimental poetry by women, and has been an artist in residence with Teachers & Writers Collaborative.

Leslie Scalapino (1944–2010) is the author of thirty books of poetry, prose inter-genre-fiction, plays, and essays. Works published in 2010 include *The Dihedrons Gazelle-Dihedrals Zoom* (The Post-Apollo Press), *Flow-Winged Crocodile and A Pair / Actions Are Erased / Appear* (Chax Press), two plays published in one volume, *The Animal is in the World like Water in Water* (Granary Books), a collaboration between Scalapino and artist Kiki Smith, and *Floats Horse-Floats or Horse-Flows* (Starcherone Books), which is a pair, or preceding volume, to *The Dihedrons Gazelle-Dihedrals Zoom.* In 2011, a revised and expanded version of her essay book *How Phenomena Appear to Unfold* (originally published by Potes & Poets in 1989) was published by Litmus Press. For more on Scalapino's life and writing, in addition to information about current projects related to her work, visit www.lesliescalapino.com.

Lyn Hejinian's most recently published book of poetry is *Saga / Circus* (2008); her new collection, *The Book of a Thousand Eyes,* will appear in 2012. She has undertaken numerous collaborative projects, including a composition titled *Quê Trân* with music by John Zorn; two mixed media books (*The Traveler and the Hill and the Hill* and *The Lake*) created with the painter Emilie Clark; the award-winning experimental documentary film *Letters Not About Love,* directed by Jacki Ochs; and *The Grand Piano: An Experiment in Collective Autobiography,* co-written with nine other poets.

Miranda Torn just turned 10 years old and lives in Manhattan and Marshall, North Carolina, with her parents and friends. She is in 4th grade and loves to read and to build things like treehouses. She has had poems published in *FOURSQUARE Magazine,* the Occupy Wall Street issue of *Critical Quarterly,* and the *Not for Mothers Only* anthology from Fence Books.

M. NourbeSe Philip is a poet, essayist, novelist, and playwright who lives in the space-time of the City of Toronto. Among her best known published works are *She Tries Her Tongue; Her Silence Softly Breaks, Looking for Livingstone: An Odyssey of Silence,* and *Harriet's Daughter,* a young adult novel. Her most recent work, *Zong!,* is a genre-breaking, book-length poem which engages with ideas of the law, history, and memory as they relate to the transatlantic slave trade.

Maria Damon teaches poetry and poetics at the University of Minnesota. She is the author of two books of poetry scholarship (*The Dark End of the Street: Margins in American Vanguard Poetry* and *Postliterary "America": from Bagel Shop Jazz to Micropoetries*), co-author (with mIEKAL aND and Jukka-Pekka Kervinen) of several online and print books of poetry; and co-editor, with Ira Livingston, of *Poetry and Cultural Studies: A Reader.*

Mark Latiner enjoys writing children's literature about monsters; fully certified, wish-granting fish fairies; and pirates who are butterflies. He hopes his stories are the kind that kids have to explain to their parents.

Marthe Reed has published two books, *Gaze* (Black Radish Books) and *Tender Box, A Wunderkammer* with drawings by Rikki Ducornet (Lavender Ink); a third book is forthcoming from Moria Books. She has also published three chapbooks, *post*cards: Lafayette a Lafayette* (with j/j hastain), *(em)bodied bliss,* and *zaum alliterations,* all as part of the Dusie Kollektiv Series. Her poetry has appeared in *New American Writing, Golden Handcuffs Review, New Orleans Review, HOW2, MiPoesias, Fairy Tale Review, Exquisite Corpse, BlazeVOX,* and *The Offending Adam,* among others.

Nicole Brodsky is the author of two poetry chapbooks—*Getting Word* and *Gestic.* She has taught both children and adults to write poetry and currently teaches writing at the University of San Francisco and San Francisco State University.

Nicole Mauro's poems and criticism have appeared in numerous publications. She is the author of seven chapbooks and one full-length poetry collection, *The Contortions* (Dusie Books, 2009), and is the co-editor of an interdisciplinary book about sidewalks titled *Intersection: Sidewalks and Public Space* (with Marci Nelligan, A'A' Arts, 2008). Her second full-length collection, *Tax-Dollar Super-Sonnet Featuring Sarah Palin as Poet* is due out 2013 (Black Radish Books). She lives in the San Francisco Bay Area with her husband, Patrick, and daughters Nina and Faye. She teaches rhetoric and language at the University of San Francisco.

Noelle Kocot: "I am the author of five books of poetry, most recently, *Poem for the End of Time and Other Poems* (Wave Books, 2006), *Sunny Wednesday* (Wave, 2009) and *The Bigger World* (Wave, 2011). I have also translated some of the poems of Tristan Corbiere from the French, and they are collected into a book called *Poet By Default* (Wave, 2011). I am the recipient of awards from The Academy of American Poets, The American Poetry Review, The Fund for Poetry, and The National Endowment for the Arts. My poems have been included in *Best American Poetry 2001* and *Best American Poetry 2012*. I live in New Jersey and teach writing in New York City."

R. Zamora Linmark is the author of three poetry collections, *Prime Time Apparitions*, *The Evolution of a Sigh*, and, most recently, *Drive-By Vigils*, all from Hanging Loose Press. He also wrote the novels *Leche* and *Rolling The R's*, which he adapted for the stage and premiered in Honolulu in 2008. He divides his writing life between San Francisco, Honolulu, and Manila.

Rachel Levitsky is the author of two book-length serial poems *Under the Sun* (Futurepoem, 2003) and *NEIGHBOR* (Ugly Duckling Presse, 2009), the experimental prose novel, *The Story of My Accident is Ours* (Futurepoem, 2012), and eight poetry and prose chapbooks. She is founder and member of Belladonna* Collaborative—a hub of feminist avant-garde literary action. She works as an Associate Professor of Writing at Pratt Institute ,where in 2010 she started, with Christian Hawkey, The Office of Recuperative Strategies: www.oors.net.

Rachel Zolf's "done" comes from *The Tolerance Project* (thetoleranceproject.blogspot.com), what could be the first collaborative MFA in Creative Writing ever. The letterpressed poem was a final project for Elaine Equi's "Minimalist Mystique" class. It contains DNA traces from Tolerance Project collaborators: Emily Beall, Joel Bettridge, Jules Boykoff, Jen Currin, Sarah Dowling, Laura Elrick, Jennifer Firestone, Lyn Hejinian, Heather Milne, Anna Moschovakis, Erín Moure, Rob Read, and Darren Wershler. Emily Beall was master of the letterpress.

Reid Gómez: "I believe we can be more beautiful than broken. Devotion to language and literature, stories and storytelling, writing and reading will restore humanity and heal severed relations. There is no alibi in being."

Robert Glück is the author of nine books of poetry and fiction, including two novels, *Margery Kempe* and *Jack the Modernist,* and a book of stories, *Denny Smith*. Glück prefaced *Between Life and Death*, a book on the paintings of Frank Moore, and he edited, along with Camille Roy, Mary Berger, and Gail Scott, the anthology *Biting The Error: Writers Explore Narrative*. Glück was Co-Director of Small Press Traffic Literary Arts Center, Director of The Poetry Center at San Francisco State, and Associate Editor at Lapis Press.

Robin Blaser was born in Denver, Colorado, in 1925 and grew up in Twin Falls, Idaho; he arrived by bus in Berkeley in 1944 where he met Jack Spicer, Robert Duncan, and many other friends. He taught at the new Simon Fraser University in Burnaby, British Columbia, for 20 years, retiring as Full Professor in 1986. In 2005 he received the Order of Canada. The University of California Press published *The Holy Forest, Collected Poems of Robin Blaser* in 2006 as well as *The Fire*, his collected essays. Robin last visited the Bay Area in November, 2008, during which he read in the Noontime Poetry Reading Series on the Berkeley Campus. This had been a lifelong wish. He died in Vancouver, Canada, on May 7, 2009. For more than 34 years, Robin shared a house on Trafalgar Street in Vancouver with his partner, David Farwell, and his dear friend from university, Ellen Tallman, and her partner, Sarah Kennedy.

Rodrigo Toscano's newest book is *Deck of Deeds* (Counterpath Press, 2012). His previous book, *Collapsible Poetics Theater*, was a 2007 National Poetry Series Selection. His writing has appeared in the anthologies *Against Expression, Diasporic Avant Gardes,* and *Best American Poetry*. Toscano works for the Labor Institute / United Steelworkers out of a laptop, tethered to a Droid, residing in airports, occupying poetics in midflight. He is based in the Greenpoint township of Brooklyn.

Rosamond S. King, Ph.D., is a poet, scholar, artist, and Auntie. Her poetry has appeared in more than a dozen anthologies, journals, and projects. She has performed in theaters and bookstores all over the world and in Aiden, Kai, and Shalini's rooms at story-time. When she's not living in the Gambia, Trinidad, or inside her own head, she is in New York City, where she is an Assistant Professor in the English Department of Brooklyn College. www.rosamondking.com.

Rosmarie Waldrop's recent poetry books are *Driven to Abstraction, Curves to the Apple, Blindsight* (New Directions), and *Love, Like Pronouns* (Omnidawn). University of Alabama Press published her collected essays, *Dissonance (if you are interested)*. Two novels, *The Hanky of Pippin's Daughter* and *A Form/of Taking/It All* are available in one paperback (Northwestern UP, 2001). She lives in Providence, Rhode Island and co-edits, with Keith Waldrop, Burning Deck books.

Sarah Anne Cox is the author of *Arrival* (Krupsaya, 2002) and *Parcel* (O Books, 2006). She was the lead artist for the project *Kindergarde*. She lives in San Francisco where she teaches, windsurfs, and cares for her two children. When not on the road, she is thinking about leaving and writing her new manuscript entitled *Medea 1-X.*

Sarah Rosenthal is the author of *Manhatten, The Animal, How I Wrote This Story, sitings,* and *not-chicago*. Her interview collection *A Community Writing Itself: Conversations with Vanguard Writers of the Bay Area* was published by Dalkey Archive in 2010. An affiliate artist at Headlands Center for the Arts from 2009 to 2011, she has received the Leo Litwak Fiction Award and grant-supported residencies at Vermont Studio Center, Soul Mountain, and Ragdale. Please visit acommunitywritingitself.com.

Sawako Nakayasu was born in Japan and has lived mostly in the U.S. since the age of six. Her most recent books are *Texture Notes* (Letter Machine Editions, 2010) and *Hurry Home Honey* (Burning Deck, 2009). She has received fellowships from the NEA and PEN, and her own work has been translated into Japanese, Norwegian, Swedish, Arabic, Chinese, and Vietnamese. More information can be found here: www.sawakonakayasu.net.

Stephanie Young lives and works in Oakland. Her most recent book, co-edited with Juliana Spahr, is *A Megaphone: Some Enactments, Some Numbers, and Some Essays about the Continued Usefulness of Crotchless-pants-and-a-machine-gun Feminism* (Chain Links, 2011). Her books of poetry are *Picture Palace* (In Girum Imus Nocte et Consumimur Igni, 2008) and *Telling the Future Off* (Tougher Disguises, 2005). She edited the anthology *Bay Poetics* and is a founding and managing editor of the interdisciplinary humanities project *Deep Oakland*.

Susan Gevirtz lives in San Francisco. Her books include *AERODROME ORION & Starry Messenger* (Kelsey Street, 2010), *BROADCAST* (Trafficker, 2009), *Thrall* (Post Apollo, 2007), *Hourglass Transcripts* (Burning Deck, 2001). *Without Event: Collected Essays* is forthcoming from Nightboat Press. She teaches at California College of the Arts and Mills College. Gevirtz has co-organized the annual translation and conversation meeting of The Paros Symposium with Greek poet Siarita Kouka and guest organizers Eleni Stecopoulos, Liana Sakelliou, and Socrates Kabouropoulos for eight years.

Susana Gardner is the author of the full-length poetry collections *HERSO* (Black Radish Books, 2011) and *[LAPSED INSEL WEARY]* (The Tangent Press, 2008). Her third book, *CADDISH*, is forthcoming from Xexoxial Editions. Her poetry has appeared in many online and print publications including *Jacket, How2, Puerto Del Sol,* and *Cambridge Literary Review* and has also been featured in several anthologies internationally. She lives in Zürich, Switzerland, where she also edits and curates the online poetics journal and experimental kollektiv press, *Dusie*.

Sweet Angelmouth is a wardrobe, set, and personal stylist with a background in songwriting, illustration, and animation. Sweet wants kids to know: "This poem is for all the other lonely kids. Things do get better. I am all grown up now, and I live in a beautiful city, have beautiful friends, and make things more beautiful for a living! Hang in there. You can do it too. Always remember to love yourself because you are the only one who knows just how beautiful you really are, from the inside out."

Tan Lin is the author of more than ten books, most recently, of *Heath Course Pak, Bib. Rev. Ed, Insominia and the Aunt,* and *7 Controlled Vocabularies and Obituary 2004. The Joy of Cooking*. He is the recipient of a 2012 Foundation for Contemporary Arts Grant, a Getty Distinguished Scholar Grant, and a Warhol Foundation/Creative Capital Arts Writing Grant to complete a book on the writings of Andy Warhol. He is working on a sampled novel, *Our Feelings Were Made By Hand*. He is an Associate Professor of English and Creative Writing at New Jersey City University.

Taylor Brady is the author of *Microclimates, Yesterday's News,* and *Occupational Treatment* and co-author with Rob Halpern of *Snow Sensitive Skin*. A new manuscript, *In the Red*, is nearing completion. He lives in Oakland, where he spends most of his time outside of writing and work learning to be a stepfather.

You already know everything about **Vanessa Place**.

A seminal figure of literary Los Angeles, **Wanda Coleman** has shared the stage with such cultural icons as Timothy Leary, Alice Coltrane, Allen Ginsberg, Bonnie Raitt, and Los Lobos. She has been a nominee for poet laureate of California and has published 18 books of poetry and fiction, which include *Bathwater Wine*, winner of the 1999 Lenore Marshall Poetry Prize—the first African-American woman to receive the award—and *Mercurochrome* (poems), bronze-medal finalist, National Book Awards 2001—both from legendary Black Sparrow Press. Now with University of Pittsburgh Press, her most recent books are *Ostinato Vamps* and *The World Falls Away*.

Will Alexander is a poet, novelist, essayist, playwright, philosopher, aphorist, and visual artist. His recent books include a book of poems, *Compression & Purity* (City Lights), a novel, *Diary As Sin* (Skylight Books), a series of plays, *Inside the Earthquake Palace* (Chax Press), and a biographical poem on Philip Lamantia, *The Brimstone Boat* (Reve a Deux). He lives in Los Angeles where he is teaching himself piano.

Writer and visual artist **Yedda Morrison** was born and raised in the San Francisco Bay Area. Her books include *Girl Scout Nation* (Displaced Press, 2008) and *Crop* (Kelsey Street Press, 2003). *Darkness (A Biocentric Reading of Joseph Conrad's Heart of Darkness)* is forthcoming from Make Now Press in Los Angeles. Morrison has exhibited her visual work throughout North America and is currently represented by Republic Gallery in Vancouver, British Coumbia. www.yeddamorrison.com.

About the *Kindergarde* Project

The idea of *Kindergarde* started with a question: What would experimental communities of writers have to say to the younger generation? What work would they create especially for children?

Small Press Traffic, a literary arts center in San Francisco, sponsored *Kindergarde* in order to find out. Small Press Traffic is uniquely open to and supportive of courageous "experimental" writing (defined in a number of ways) and outsider publishing traditions. SPT is also interested in seeing these occupy a less marginalized place in the culture at large, especially works that interrogate issues of social justice and equity. Believing that a culturally diverse avant-garde is key to a relevant American literature and offering an alternative to mainstream publishing and poetics, Small Press Traffic encourages exploration and experimentation and was eager to support *Kindergarde*.

In 2009, Small Press Traffic received a Creative Work Fund Grant to commission experimental literary work for this children's anthology. In April and May of the following year, performances of some of the *Kindergarde* pieces were held at California College of the Arts, the Bay Area Discovery Museum, and the Museum of Children's Art in Oakland, complete with live trombonist accompaniment. Chris Smith, former Artistic Director of the Magic Theater, directed the performances, and Patrick Maloney, a Bay Area visual artist and arts advocate, designed the costumes and sets. The performances also included a number of talented, professional actors— Cyril Jamal Cooper, Caleb Haven Draper, Juliet Heller, Mandy Khoshnevisan, Norman Muñoz, Andy Strain, and Shaye Troha—who brought the pieces to life. Peter Merts photo documented the project from start to finish, and Skip Brown videotaped the performances.

In taking on the project of *Kindergarde*, Small Press Traffic hoped to:

- Expand children's awareness of the power of language and trigger their imaginations in fresh ways;

- Offer young people alternative views of what poetry/story/performance can look like and be (both through the "Poets' Theater" events and the *Kindergarde* anthology;

- Encourage the creation and reception of new experimental work specifically for children by nationally recognized avant-garde poets and writers from the Bay Area and other parts of the country; and

- Support collaboration between artists in many disciplines and communities and those affiliated with the organization's experimental writing communities.

Kindergarde invited experimental writers from all over the country to re-create their poetics and ideas for younger audiences in order to see what this community of writers would say to children. The *Kindergarde* anthology is the result of this effort. Many thanks to the Creative Work Fund for making this project possible. We are grateful for their generous support.

Kindergarde performance of Robin Blaser's poems at California College of the Arts in April, 2010. Back row: Cyril Jamal Cooper, Shaye Troha, Caleb Haven Draper, and Juliet Heller; front row: Mandy Khoshnevisan and Norman Muñoz

Kindergarde performance at California College of the Arts in April, 2010; Andy Strain's trombone blew kids away

Shaye Troha and Mandy Khoshnevisan sporting Patrick Maloney's whimsical *Kindergarde* costumes at the Museum of Children's Art in Oakland (April, 2010)

The *Kindergarde* Performance Team

Director: Chris Smith is a producer and director. He was founding Artistic Director of the Obie Award-winning Youngblood (NYC), Artistic Director of the Magic Theatre (SF), and Interim Executive Director of the Napa Valley Opera House. He has directed dozens of plays, Off-Broadway and regionally, and currently is Chief Operating Officer of BlueRare Productions. Chris is a graduate of Brown University and lives with his family in Marin.

Costume & Set Designer: Patrick Maloney has been making things since childhood. After graduating from San Jose State College, he worked as an illustrator in advertising and publishing and then moved on to making sculpture and painting. He has been teaching for more than 20 years at San Quentin State Prison and has also been working with young people in Marin County. Patrick received an award for his work in Community Arts from the Marin Community Foundation in 2002.

Photographer: Peter Merts grew up in Georgia, received a liberal arts education at Duke University, and has lived in the San Francisco area for over 35 years. He has been photographing for 30 years, working mostly on long-term fine arts and documentary projects. Most recently he has been documenting the practice of the fine arts by inmates of the California prison system.

Acknowledgements

The editor and publisher would like to thank the following writers and presses for their permission to reprint the poems, plays, stories, and songs in this anthology:

Anne Waldman, "Manatee/Humanity" from *Manatee/Humanity* (Penguin, 2009). Copyright © 2009 by Anne Waldman. Used by permission of the author.

Bruce Covey, "Circles" from *Glass Is Really a Liquid* (No Tell Books, 2010). Copyright © 2010 by Bruce Covey. Used by permission of the author.

CA Conrad, "(Soma)tic Poetry Exercise: Shopping Mall Trees" from *A BEAUTIFUL MARSUPIAL AFTERNOON: New (Soma)tics* (WAVE Books, 2012). Copyright © 2012 by CA Conrad. Used by permission of the author.

Cathy Park Hong, "Hula Hooper's Taunt" from *Dance Dance Revolution* (W. W. Norton & Company, 2008). Copyright © 2008 by Cathy Park Hong. Used by permission of the author.

Charles Bernstein, "Emma's Nursery Rimes" from *Girly Man* (University of Chicago Press, 2006). Copyright © 2006 by Charles Bernstein. Used by permission of the author.

Donna de la Perrière, "Surface Tension" from *True Crime* (Talisman, 2009). Copyright © 2009 by Donna de la Perrière. Used by permission of the author.

Edwin Torres, "THE NAME OF THINGS" from *Yes Thing No Thing* (Roof Books, 2010). Copyright © 2010 by Edwin Torres. Used by permission of the author.

Elizabeth Treadwell, "fairly cwen" from *Virginia or the mud-flap girl* (Dusie Press, 2012). Copyright © 2012 by Elizabeth Treadwell. Used by permission of the author.

Eillen Myles, "Jacaranda" from *Sorry, Tree* (Wave Books, 2007). Copyright © 2007 by Eileen Myles. Used by permission of the author.

giovanni singleton, "bird" from *Ascension* (Counterpath Press, 2011). Copyright © 2011 by giovanni singleton. Used by permission of the author.

Harryette Mullen, "Wipe that Smile Off Your Aphasia" from *Sleeping with the Dictionary* (University of California Press, 2002). Copyright © 2002 by Harryette Mullen. Used by permission of the author.

Joan Larkin, "IF YOU WERE GOING TO GET A PET" first published in *Tarpaulin Sky* (Spring, 2003). Copyright © 2003 by Joan Larkin. Used by permission of the author.

Julien Poirier, "Moon Lion" from *El Golpe Chileño* (Ugly Duckling Books, 2010). Copyright © 2010 by Julien Poirier. Used by permission of the author.

Leslie Scalapino, "The Plane," "Gemsbox," and "Breath-memory" from *The Dihedrons Gazelle-Dihedrals Zoom* (The Post-Apollo Press, 2010). Copyright © 2010 by Leslie Scalapino. Used by permission of the author.

M. NourbeSe Philip, "Zong #17" from *Zong!* (Wesleyan, 2008). Copyright © 2008 by M. NourbeSe Philip. Used by permission of the author.

Maria Damon, "Respect" from *Meshwards* (Dusie Kollektiv, 2010). Copyright © 2010 by Maria Damon. Used by permission of the author.

Marthe Reed, "Canon: a strange loop" from tender box, *a wunderkammer* (Lavender Ink, 2007). Copyright © 2007 by Marthe Reed. Used by permission of the author.

Rachel Levitsky, excerpt from "Basement, Basement, Window" from *Renoemos* (delete press, 2009). Copyright © 2009 by Rachel Levitsky. Used by permission of the author.

Sawako Nakayasu, "7.9.2003" from *Texture Notes* (Letter Machine Editions, 2010). Copyright © 2010 by Sawako Nakayasu. Used by permission of the author.

Susana Gardner, "Shores" from HERSO (Black Radish Books, 2011). Copyright © 2011 by Susana Gardner. Used by permission of the author.

Wanda Coleman, "COFFEE" from *African Sleeping Sickness: Stories & Poems* (Black Sparrow Press, 1990). Copyright © 1990 by Wanda Coleman. Used by permission of the author.

Will Alexander, excerpt from *Across The Vapor Gulf* (Aligatorzine, 2010). Copyright © 2010 by Will Alexander. Used by permission of the author.

Thanks to the following photographers for the use of their work in *Kindergarde*:

Front cover, from top: jim barber/Bigstock.com, Eric Isselée/Bigstock.com, Maksym Bondarchuk/Bigstock.com, Dee Golden/Bigstock.com, Steve Byland/Bigstock.com, Jacob Hamblin/Bigstock.com; pg. 9: Samantha Grandy/Bigstock.com; pg. 17: Daniel Hurst/Bigstock.com; pg. 18: Ivan Kmit/Bigstock.com; pg. 30: Eric Isselée/Bigstock.com; pg. 31, from top: Donald Swartz/Bigstock.com, Jacob Hamblin/Bigstock.com; pg. 32: Fabian Schmidt/Bigstock.com; pg. 33: Ivan Kmit/Bigstock.com; pg. 34, from top: Oleg Iatsun/Bigstock.com, Sergey Kotlikov/Bigstock.com; pg. 49: Ljupco Smokovski/Bigstock.com; pg. 50: J.A.G. Sandvik/Bigstock.com; pg. 61: Barbara Helgason/Bigstock.com; pg. 62: Achim Prill/Bigstock.com; pg. 63, from top: Ioannis Syrigos/Bigstock.com, Jim Barber/Bigstock.com, Andrey Eremin/Bigstock.com; pg. 65: Paul Radulescu/Bigstock.com; pg. 66, from top: dimitris kolyris/Bigstock.com, Tim/Bigstock.com; pg. 69: Mau Horng/Bigstock.com; pg. 77: Shirokov Alexander Leonidovich/Bigstock.com; pg. 78: Vince Clements/Bigstock.com; pg. 82: Madlen/Bigstock.com; pg. 85: Kim Reinick/Bigstock.com; pg. 86: Maksym Bondarchuk/Bigstock.com; pg. 90: Yong Hian Lim/Bigstock.com; pg. 92: Sergey Galushko/Bigstock.com; pg. 93: Santiago Cornejo/Bigstock.com; pg. 96: Dykun Andriy/Bigstock.com; pg. 98: Sascha Burkard/Bigstock.com; pg. 108: Luis Francisco Cordero/Bigstock.com; pg. 109: Valentyn Volkov/Bigstock.com; pg. 110: Aleksey Sysoev/Bigstock.com; pg. 111: Le Do/Bigstock.com; pgs. 113 & 114: Mike Kiev; pg. 115, from top: Carolina K. Smith, M.D./Bigstock.com, Eric Isselée/Bigstock.com; pg. 121: ivan montero/Bigstock.com; pg. 126: Vladimir Yudin/Bigstock.com; pg. 127: gavran333/Bigstock.com; pg. 138: Alexander Potapov/Bigstock.com; pg. 139: Nikolai Sorokin/Bigstock.com; pg. 140: Marek Chalupnik/Bigstock.com; pg. 146: Eric Broder Van Dyke/Bigstock.com; pg. 149: Laurent Renault/Bigstock.com; pg. 150: Dee Golden/Bigstock.com; pg. 151: Brooke Becker/Bigstock.com; pg. 152, from top: Richard Carey/Bigstock.com, Life On White/Bigstock.com; pg. 158: Ian Klein/Bigstock.com; pg. 159, from top: Daniel Hurst/Bigstock.com, Irina Tischenko/Bigstock.com; pg. 161: Paul Fleet/Bigstock.com; pg. 163: Robert Spriggs/Bigstock.com, pg. 178: dan ionut popescu/Bigstock.com; back cover: Ivan Kmit/Bigstock.com

About the Editor

Dana Teen Lomax is a mom and a poet. She started writing poetry when she was in 4th grade and has written and edited several books since then. Her poetry has received California Arts Council, Marin Arts Council, San Francisco Foundation, and other awards. She has taught writing in many different places, including universities, elementary, middle, and high schools, juvenile detention centers, hospitals, and prisons. Currently, Dana teaches at San Francisco State University and with California Poets in the Schools. She lives with her family near San Francisco, along with their two cats—Jacko Riley and Carrot—and their incredible dog, Windy.

SEE YOU LATER